P. G. Hamerton

The etcher's handbook

Giving an account of the old processes, and of processes recently discovered

P. G. Hamerton

The etcher's handbook
Giving an account of the old processes, and of processes recently discovered

ISBN/EAN: 9783742826817

Manufactured in Europe, USA, Canada, Australia, Japa

Cover: Foto ©Andreas Hilbeck / pixelio.de

Manufactured and distributed by brebook publishing software (www.brebook.com)

P. G. Hamerton

The etcher's handbook

THE
ETCHER'S HANDBOOK.

BY

PHILIP GILBERT HAMERTON,

AUTHOR OF "ETCHING AND ETCHERS."

GIVING AN ACCOUNT OF THE OLD PROCESSES, AND OF
PROCESSES RECENTLY DISCOVERED.

ILLUSTRATED BY THE AUTHOR.

"What, then, is the amount and kind of previous knowledge and skill required by the etcher? It is an innate artistic spirit, without which all the study in the world is useless. It is the cultivation of this spirit, not arduously but lovingly. It is the knowledge that is acquired by a life of devotion to what is true and beautiful —by the daily and hourly habit of weighing and comparing what we see in nature, and the thinking of how it should be represented in art. It is the habit of constant observation of great things and small, and the experience that springs from it. It is taste, which a celebrated painter once said, but not truly, is rarer than genius. The skill that grows out of these habits is the skill required by the etcher. It is the skill of the analyst and of the synthesist—the skill to combine, and the skill to separate—to compound and to simplify—to detach plane from plane—to fuse detail into mass—to subordinate definition to space, distance, light, and air. Finally, it is the acumen to perceive the near relationship that expression bears to form, and the skill to draw them—not separately, but together."

From an Article in the Fine Arts Quarterly Review by MR. SEYMOUR HADEN.

SECOND EDITION.

CHARLES ROBERSON & CO.
99, LONG ACRE, LONDON.
1875.

CONTENTS.

	PAGE
Preface	v.

Chapter I.
The Old Negative Process with Stopping-out ... 1

Chapter II.
The Old Negative Process avoiding Stopping-out . 10

Chapter III.
Lalanne's Doctrine about Lines . . 13

Chapter IV.
Haden's Doctrine about the Etched Line . 15

Chapter V.
Soft Ground Etching . . . 19

Chapter VI.
Bracquemond's Pen Process 21

Chapter VII.
Hamerton's Brush Process . . . 23

Chapter VIII.
Haden's Negative Process 26

Chapter IX.
Hamerton's Negative Process . . . 32

Chapter X.
Hamerton's Positive Process 36

Chapter XI.
On the Etching Needle or Point . . 44

CONTENTS.

	PAGE
CHAPTER XII.	
The Dry Point . . .	45
CHAPTER XIII.	
To Efface Faulty Passages	47
CHAPTER XIV.	
To Reduce a Passage that is Overbitten	48
CHAPTER XV.	
Etching from Nature . . .	49
CHAPTER XVI.	
Etchings to be Studied	55
CHAPTER XVII.	
The Training of an Etcher	64
CHAPTER XVIII.	
Vulgar Errors about Etching . . .	68
CHAPTER XIX.	
Printing	78
CHAPTER XX.	
Some Notes on Etching Tools . .	81
CHAPTER XXI.	
The Illustrations	83
CHAPTER XXII.	
Of Finish in Etching . . .	92
ADDENDA .	93

PREFACE.

ALTHOUGH the new processes in etching may be expected in a great measure to supersede those which have been handed down to us by our predecessors in the art, I have thought it best, for several reasons, to give an equally full account of all of them.

It happens, in the first place, that the most revolutionary of these processes is a discovery of my own, and as inventors are always liable to be suspected of undue partiality to their own inventions, the best way to escape suspicions of this kind seemed to be that of treating all processes which have at any time led to good results on a footing of strict equality. Again, although some etchers may like the new processes, others with equally good reason may prefer to remain faithful to the old ones. This is a matter to be decided by the temperament of each practitioner for himself, and the writer of a handbook on the art fulfils his duty best in offering his readers the widest possible range for choice. And the same etcher may find it convenient to resort to different processes at different times, according to the need of the occasion. The student will therefore do wisely to choose his process according to his taste and temper, and also according to the need of the hour. And let him be assured of this, that unless he really likes the process that he uses, and heartily enjoys the work whilst he is doing it, there is not the faintest chance, whatever his knowledge and ability as an artist, that he will produce a good etching, or anything resembling a good etching. All cold or dull, or business-like etching, however clever and scientific it may be, bears the same relation to the real thing that verse-making does to poetry. And just as a poet, when he sits down to write a lyric, ought not to be bothered with ink and pens of a kind which do not suit him, and are likely to fret him and put him out of temper, so every etcher ought studiously to avoid those varnishes and acids whose operation does not seem to him convenient.

The reader to whom etching is a new subject is especially warned not to judge of the capabilities of the art by the general mass of modern production, which is quite unworthy of his attention. There are a few good living etchers, but very few; and out of the quantities of etchings which are published every year, nine out of ten are not only valueless, but a nuisance, doing much harm by propagating and confirming the false conceptions of the art which are generally prevalent. The majority of amateurs seem to imagine that drawing and chiaroscuro of a degree of badness which nobody would tolerate in a picture, somehow become allowable in an etching; that because good etchings are usually free, an etcher is at liberty to set at defiance all the known laws of nature and of art; that the mere act of drawing on varnished copper implies of itself a mysterious cleverness, elevating the practitioner above the common canons of art-criticism. On the other hand, those of our artists who could really etch if they liked are so busy making fortunes with the brush that they have hardly any leisure for a less remunerative pursuit.

I would ask the reader to think of etching simply as a kind of highly-concentrated drawing, subject to the same laws as any other kind of point-drawing,* but more difficult to execute because complicated

---

* Except that more artistic feeling is expected from an etcher than from any other artist, because the best etchers have always concentrated so much passionate expression in their work with the etching-needle.

(whatever process you employ) by calculations about biting. And the first step towards becoming an etcher is to become a good draughtsman with any pointed instrument. The second step is to master the relations of light and dark in nature. The third and final stage of an etcher's education is to obtain a technical mastery over copper, so as to make the copper yield the precise tone he requires, whether in the depth of a single line or in the shading of a space. Few modern etchers have mastered the copper in this way; they do not give time enough to the art. It may be done, however, by great labour. Jacquemart and Martial have, each of them, subdued the copper, as Joachim has subdued the violin, the difficulty being probably very nearly equal in both of these two great expressional fine arts.

THE ETCHER'S HANDBOOK.

CHAPTER I.

The Old Negative Process

WITH STOPPING OUT.

1. CLEANING THE PLATE.

Before the artist laid his ground the plate was cleaned with turpentine and whitening. The whitening was afterwards removed with bread.

2. THE GROUND.

The etching ground was composed of white wax, bitumen, pitch, and resin. Sometimes one of the ingredients was omitted, but never the white wax. Sometimes gum-mastic was used instead of resin.

Bosse's ground was composed of white wax 30 grammes, gum-mastic 30 gr., asphaltum 15 gr.

It is not exactly known what was the composition of the ground Rembrandt *used*, but an old ground which bears his name is as follows:—White wax 30 gr., gum-mastic 15 gr., asphaltum or amber 15 gr. The mastic and asphaltum were pounded separately in a mortar. The wax was melted in a glazed earthen pot, and the other ingredients were added little by little, the operator stirring all the time.

Callot's ground was composed as follows:—White

wax 60 gr., amber or asphaltum 60 gr., gum-mastic from 30 to 60 gr., according to the heat of the weather, the hotter the weather the more gum-mastic, which was the hardening ingredient.

Several other grounds used by the old masters have been handed down to us, and the reader who is curious on these subjects will find a fuller account of them in 'Etching and Etchers.' It is enough to explain here the principle common to all these compositions, which is simply to get hardness or softness, at will, by the addition of a hard or a soft ingredient.

Again, it is necessary that the ground should behave well under the dabber, not *sticking* to it, or else it cannot be spread evenly. Also its constitution must be such that it will take smoke without losing quality.

If the student has any difficulty in preparing a ground, he will probably overcome the difficulty by altering the proportions of the ingredients in obedience to these principles.

Let him remember always that the quality of a ground depends very much upon temperature, that a ground which will shell off the plate on a cold day may be the very thing you want on a hot one. Hence a knowing etcher mixes his ground with some reference to the season. It may be observed, however, that the soft grounds do fairly well in most weathers, provided you do not touch them, but use a hand-rest, whereas the hard grounds are so liable to become unsafe when the temperature is in the least below what is suitable for them, that it is always safer to err on the side of softness—that is of the wax ingredient —than on that of hardness, or the resinous ingredient.

When the ground is thoroughly mixed, you pour it into tepid water and roll it into balls.

3. TO LAY THE GROUND.

Wrap a ball of ground in new taffetas silk, of a kind from which small particles do not detach themselves.

Fasten a hand-vice to the margin of the plate, inserting a piece of cardboard to prevent it from roughening the copper.

Heat the plate over a spirit-lamp or anything else, provided there is no dust.

The degree of heat must be enough to melt the composition, but not enough to burn it. The composition, when melted on the plate, *must not boil*. If you burn your ground it will crack off under the point, and so any work you do upon it will be useless and worthless.

When the plate is properly heated, the ground will melt through the silk and spread itself easily as you pass the ball over the plate.

Very likely there will be a sort of greasiness or repulsion in the copper in spite of all your cleaning, so that the ground will avoid the copper in parts, as ink avoids greasy paper. Do not let this discourage you. The ground will spread itself properly under the dabber, and if the dabber does not accomplish this quite perfectly, a subsequent operation will.

4. THE DABBER.

You now need the dabber, which is made of cotton-wool and horse-hair, covered with silk, and kept in shape by a disc of cardboard. To make a dabber you lay first the cotton-wool on the silk, then the horsehair on that, then the disc of cardboard on the horsehair, and finally, you bring the silk up on all sides round the disc, bind it with cord, and cut off what is superfluous, leaving just enough to hold it by.

5. DABBING THE GROUND.

Whilst the plate is still heated, you dab the ground all over it with the dabber, to spread it evenly.

If this is well done, the ground will be thinly and evenly spread, and of a pale golden colour, showing the shine of the copper well through it.

If you have too much, you may clean the dabber on a piece of coarse canvas (like that used for printing) and dab again, cleaning the dabber repeatedly, whilst you are at work. In this way the superfluous ground is easily removed.

If you have not enough ground, add a little from the ball and dab again.

6. SMOKING THE GROUND.

Still holding the plate with the hand-vice, heat it again, but not so as to burn the ground.

Whilst the plate is hot, hold it up in the air, the covered side down, and expose it to the smoke of wax tapers, twisted together.

The flame should just touch the plate, no more, and should be passed rapidly along its surface, never resting at one place, or else it would burn it. If this is properly done, the smoke-black will incorporate itself with the ground all over the plate, and produce a beautiful black surface.

7. QUALITY OF THE SMOKE.

Much depends upon the quality of the smoke. That from wax is good; that from mineral oils is abundant, but too greasy, and the ground does not harden well with it.

8. BURNING THE GROUND.

As I have already warned the reader, a ground which is burned anywhere will shell off when you come to etch upon it, or if not then, it is liable to shell off afterwards in the bath. Hard grounds behave worse when burned than soft grounds do.

If you discover afterwards, when at work, that a portion of your ground, which you believed to be sound, is burnt, you may sometimes get over the difficulty by using a sharper point. A ground which will shell off with a blunt point will often bear work with a sharp one.

9. BANKING THE PLATE.

As I am describing the old process of etching quite faithfully, I am bound to give an account of banking the plate, one of the most unnecessary of traditional processes, and at the same time one of the most troublesome.

It never seems to have occurred to the old etchers that if they could protect one side of the plate against acid, they could protect the other side too, so they took the trouble to build a hedge of wax all round the margin of the plate in order to make a bath of it to receive the acid.

"Banking-wax" was composed of beeswax mixed with resin. It was usually *kept* in sticks, but before being used these sticks were put into warm water and flattened out between the fingers, till they were like ribands. These ribands of wax being set on edge all round the plate, and joined together where they met, made a wall round it, and they were pressed to the plate to make them stick. It was a tradition that they were to be pressed with a very hot key (just as a very cold key applied to the back of the neck is said to cure hiccup), probably because some early practitioner of the art had happened to have nothing better by him, and had got into the habit of using a key for the purpose. Then the wall of wax was painted with varnish to prevent the acid getting out. Very often, however, it did get out, notwithstanding all these precautions.

The old etchers never reflected how much simpler it would have been just to lay the ground on *both* sides of the plate, and plunge it bodily into a flat bath. It is only, I believe, since photographers took to using flat trays for baths that etchers have learned to use them also.

I very well remember, in my first attempts at etching (made twenty-two years ago), the trouble I had with "banking-wax."

Even in the case of the very largest engravers' plates, there is not the least necessity for banking-wax, as porcelain trays can now be had of a large size.

10. ETCHING.

The custom of the old etchers seems to have been to do all the work at once with the point, or nearly so, except what came in the way of corrections and finishing with the Dry Point. How they managed to get paler and deeper tones in the biting will be seen shortly.

11. BITING.

The plate being banked all round with wax had

acid poured upon it. The acid used was most commonly nitric, mixed with an equal volume of water. Other mixtures are said to have been used by the old masters, but the best mordant known to them was the nitric mordant.*

The mordant was left on the plate just long enough to bite the *palest* tones only. Then it was poured off, and the plate dried. Then the passages which were to remain pale were painted over with stopping-out varnish.

Here is an old receipt for stopping-out varnish, but Brunswick black is used now instead of it:—

White wax 8 grammes, asphaltum 30 gr., gum-mastic 4 gr., turpentine 240 gr.

12. BITING, *continued*.

The stopping-out varnish being applied, and having dried, the acid was again poured upon the plate. When it had bitten some time longer, it was taken out again and stopped again, and so on, till the darkest lines were deep enough.

13. OBJECTIONS TO STOPPING-OUT.

Stopping-out is a troublesome and objectionable process, both because it takes a great deal of time, also causing delay in waiting for drying, and because, however much pains you take, it cannot always be done delicately enough. For instance, it is all but impossible to stop out passages of much intricacy, such as a sky seen between the branches of a tree.

I remember distinctly that when I practised the old

---

* This mordant takes from five minutes for the palest lines to half-an-hour for the darkest, in temperate weather.

process some plates cost me more time and trouble in stopping-out than in the drawing of the subject on the copper.

14. RE-BITING.

If the artist found the subject insufficiently bitten, he cleaned the plate very carefully with turpentine and whitening, and bread, and proceeded to cover the whole of the *smooth* surface with etching ground by means of a dabber, which took it up evenly from another plate. He then put his banking-wax round the plate again, and gave it a second biting.

Contemporary etchers use a roller for this purpose instead of a dabber, as it is more certain, but the roller is of use only when the plate is perfectly flat.

15. OBJECTIONS TO RE-BITING.

The ground fills up the pale lines, and only leaves those which are already deep to be re-bitten. Thus the process alters the relations of the lines already made, and that in a manner necessarily different from the first intention of the artist.

A plate which has been re-bitten has usually an unequal look, caused by the excessive depth of the deep lines. The pale lines look, by contrast, paler after the operation than they did before it.

Re-biting has been largely resorted to by the proprietors of old worn coppers by great masters. Very many of Rembrandt's coppers (which still exist) have been re-bitten, and such re-biting always spoils them by giving a violently disproportionate accent to certain lines.

Of course re-biting may be occasionally used by an intelligent etcher with advantage, to give additional weight to heavy foreground lines, but it can never revive a weak plate equally.

16. TRANSPARENT GROUNDS.

When a plate requires additional work it may be covered with a transparent ground, which shows the work already done, and then the artist may add what he likes.

Here is a receipt for an old transparent ground said to be Rembrandt's.

White wax 30 grammes, gum-mastic 15 gr., asphaltum or amber, 15 gr. Melt the wax first, and add the other ingredients gradually, in powder.

A more convenient transparent ground will be found amongst the new processes.

17. DRY POINT.

The old etchers very often finished their plates in dry point. As the use of the dry point is never likely to become antiquated, it will be dwelt upon at length elsewhere.

Note.—When you use stopping-out at all, give plenty of time to it, and remember this maxim, handed down to us from the elder etchers:—"*One day of stopping-out is worth five with the needle.*"

CHAPTER II.

The Old Negative Process,

AVOIDING STOPPING-OUT.

1. THE FIRST BITING.

Having grounded and smoked your plate in the old-fashioned way (*see* Old Process, pp. 3 & 4), you first trace your subject, which may be easily done by rubbing the back of a drawing with chalk, and then having laid it on the grounded plate passing over the principal lines with a blunt point. You then etch all those parts, and those only, which are to be darkest, such as vigorous foreground work in landscapes, and any black and deep markings wherever you may happen to want them.

Use a blunt point for this work and keep the lines well open. Admit no delicate lines at this stage. Work as Turner did in his etched foregrounds, at least on his principle, making few lines, but these few all strongly suggestive of the light-and-shade of the composition, no outlines, as such, only the darkest places marked by bold marks, leaving the outlines to take care of themselves.

If the reader cares to follow the old tradition of etching to the letter, he will now *bank* his plate with banking-wax, but if he prefers convenience to tradition

THE NEGATIVE PROCESS.

he will japan the back of it, and the place where the hand-vice was fixed, and then use a porcelain bath.

The plate is to be immersed in the acid bath long enough to produce very black lines, say half-an-hour, in the usual nitric bath. Then clean it, and have a proof taken to guide you in subsequent labours.

2. THE SECOND BITING.

Ground your plate again and smoke it. The deep lines will still be very clearly visible, notwithstanding the black ground.

With the proof before you, draw all work that is to be neither very dark nor yet pale. Employ for this purpose a point sharper than before, but not yet quite sharp. Let your lines be nearer to each other than they were, yet not close.

Immerse your plate a second time in the bath till it is bitten sufficiently to make the lines moderately deep. Remove it, clean it, and take a second proof.

3. THE THIRD BITING.

You now ground with transparent ground, and do not smoke. Proceed with all pale and delicate work, such as distances, skies, &c., and with pale tones in near objects, such as tender shades in fur of white animals, &c., and with pale tones that have to cover whole spaces where work has been already done, but which require to be veiled with what painters would call a scumble or a glase.

This is not so easy as when you worked in the black ground, because you will not see your lines very distinctly.

In the third etching you must keep the lines close to each other, and use a sharp needle, provided your needle be not sharp enough to make little involuntary stoppages on the copper, jumping from one point to another.

4. ADVANTAGES OF THIS PROCESS.

The advantages of this process are considerable. First, by the clear analysis and division of the work to be done you know what lies before you, and by taking proofs during the progress of your plate, you ensure in a great measure the safety of its progress. By referring to the proofs, you perceive what remains to be done. The system of separate bitings is a considerable element of safety.

A technical advantage of very great importance is the facility with which, by this process, you may introduce pale lines amongst darker ones. For instance, if you have drawn a tree with dark, intricate branches in your foreground, you may introduce a delicate distance or sky as seen between the branches by simply etching, in the third process, as if they did not exist, whereas to manage the same effect by stopping out, would be tedious in the extreme. In the same manner you may subdue glaring and obnoxious lights by throwing a delicate tint over them, still preserving the full importance of the vigorous lines.

In connection with this process, the reader is requested to take note of the chapter which follows.

CHAPTER III.

Lalanne's Doctrine about Lines.

M. LALANNE, the eminent French etcher, has first given definite shape and expression to a doctrine about lines, which is founded on certain technical necessities, and on the practice of the most successful etchers. The student ought therefore to know this doctrine, and remember it when he works, but not to give it a too rigid or formal obedience, because in art the very best of doctrines (and this is one of the best) are liable to become hindrances to the free development of individual ability. An artist ought to know all the best maxims about his art, and yield them an intelligent obedience just so long as they are of use to him, but not one minute longer.

M. Lalanne's doctrine is this:

Lines which are to be deeply bitten ought to be kept apart from each other; those which are to be of medium depth ought to be nearer; and very shallow lines ought to be quite close to each other. To express the doctrine in a concentrated form:—*The breadth of the white spaces between the lines ought to be in proportion to the depth of the biting.*

To inexperienced etchers, or even to experienced ones who have not much observation, this doctrine of Lalanne always appears a bit of capricious dogmatism. It may therefore be well to explain the reason for it.

I cannot tell you why, but it is a fact that biting

always sets in soonest where the lines are nearest together.

Consequently, if you want any one biting to go on evenly, the lines exposed during that biting must be tolerably equi-distant. There must not be very close work in one place and very open work in another place. The close places would be deeply bitten before the solitary lines were even attacked.

Again, as the more open the work is, the longer it takes for the biting to get fairly to work all over it, the most open work must be longest exposed to the action of the acid.

Finally, in landscape, it is the distances which are to be palest. The eye is best satisfied to find close and delicate work in a distance.

The reason for this will be easily understood. Suppose you see any set of equally-sized objects, the upright bars of an iron railing, for instance, as the rails of the garden of the Tuileries, vanishing in a long perspective: the nearer they are the more open they are, and the thicker each appears; the more they recede in distance the closer they are, and the thinner each appears. So it is with natural objects, the ripples in water, the stems of trees in a forest, men in a street, &c. The continual, though unconscious observation of this fact, makes us associate the idea of distance with thinness combined with closeness, and the idea of nearness with thickness combined with openness.

Hence the reader will perceive that M. Lalanne's theory, like all sound theories about art, is based upon the observation of nature, and our habits of mental association, even though at first it may seem to have nothing to do with nature.

CHAPTER IV.

Haden's Doctrine about the Etched Line.

THE distinguished English etcher, Mr. Seymour Haden advocates a doctrine about the line distinct from that of Lalanne, which equally deserves the student's attention.

Mr. Haden's doctrine is, that the etched line, being on account of its extreme and even unrivalled obedience to the slightest variations in the will or sentiment of the artist, precious in the highest degree as a means of artistic expression, ought to be frankly shown and not dissimulated, except under circumstances where its vital accents are unnecessary.

The difference between this doctrine and the ordinary feeling, both of painters and the public, is very great. A painter, from his habit of working in a medium which excludes the line altogether, and deals only with graduated spaces, has usually a feeling of embarrassment about the line, and a desire to hide it as much as possible under graduated tones. In a word, many painters, especially of the English school, attempt to paint with the point rather than etch with it. In the kind of work they do they are often eminently successful. Hook, for example, and Frederick Tayler, are both of them accomplished painters with the point. So also in another way is Samuel Palmer, whose etchings are most perfect and admirable examples of the rich and full quality they aim at.

For my own part, though fully recognizing the fine tone and clever drawing of the best members of the English etching club, I believe Haden's doctrine to be the right one, namely, that the line ought to be preserved as much as possible, and made the most of. I think that as painting depends upon tones, and it would be a barbarism to introduce lines in that art, so since etching begins with the line, which the etching-needle draws in the ground, it would be barbarous to affect to ignore it, and imitate other arts, such as mezzotint in which there are no lines. Every art does best when it is *most itself*. Of course we all know that there are no lines in nature, but all art is conventional, more or less, very much as language is (even painting is much more conventional than people generally imagine), so the most honest way appears to be that which confesses the conventionalism most frankly. And though the line does not exist in nature, it often explains, suggests, and interprets nature far more clearly and vividly than anything else would in the same time. There is an anecdote of Turner, to the effect that, having once taken a memorandum in water-colour, he said to a friend near him, "How much more I should have got with the pencil-point!" Yes, a line will often tell more about a form than could be expressed with much more labour by colouring a space, and there is a sort of language in the linear arts which enables the artist to convey a good deal to an intelligent person already acquainted with that kind of language, which to another would remain unintelligible. No genuine etcher would ever pretend that his art was an imitation of nature, it is an interpretation, not an imitation. And although nature cannot be deceptively imitated by lines, lines are most efficient in the interpretation of nature.

Now, an etched line is of all engraved lines the most free; it offers slighter hindrances to the immediate mental expression than any other engraved line can; indeed it is so perfectly free as to offer no appreciable delay or obstacle of any kind whatever. The slightest accent or deviation, even the most transient hesitation or trembling of the designer's hand, is at once registered by the sensitive line. In a word, the line is *vital* from beginning to end, and as the eye follows it, it reads the varying thoughts and moods of the artist. To sacrifice all this vitality by hiding the line is to incur a most serious loss, which cannot, in this art, be compensated. In painting there are no lines, but then there is the brushwork, which is often, in the highest degree, expressive of the artist's feeling, and therefore which serves the same purpose as the expressive line in etching. In etching, if you sacrifice the linear expression, you have no *executive* expression left, you have no brushwork to take its place, you are working with a point and not with a brush, and you must have *point*-expression, that is, *line*-expression or none. A stupid (or else malevolent) critic in one of the daily papers tried to make it appear that I undervalued painting in insisting upon the value of the etched line, but if I were writing about painting I should insist just as emphatically on the value of manly and visible brushwork deliberately left undisturbed. The greatest painter-etcher who ever lived, Rembrandt, used his brush as honestly as his etching-point, and his etching-point as honestly as his brush. Whether he painted or etched, there was never the least dissimulation of the means used, because, whichever of the two arts he practised, he knew the value of *executive expression*, that kind of expression by which the hand, from the beginning of the work to the end of it, reveals the most delicately various phases of passing emotion, the seekings, and waitings, and hesitations, and the bursts of passionate ardour when the light from heaven flashes upon the soul of the artist, and his heart glows with tenfold heat, and the hand cannot be swift enough to record what the brain sees in the intensity of the inward vision.

CHAPTER V.

Soft Ground Etching.

IN this kind of etching a skilful artist, accustomed to the process, can produce a very close imitation of pencil-drawing.

You take a ball of ordinary etching-ground and mix it with an equal quantity of tallow, heating both ingredients and stirring till the mixture is quite perfect. In hot weather use less tallow, because that is the softening ingredient, and you require most of it in cold weather.

Make fresh balls of the mixture, and enclose them in a covering of fine taffetas silk. Then lay your ground on the plate and smoke it, as in the former process.

This being done, take care, in the first place, not to touch the plate with your fingers, as that would remove the ground. Then take a paper with a certain amount of roughness in its texture, but not a thick paper, moisten one side of it, and stretch your paper over the plate, exactly as you would stretch paper on a drawing board for water colour, turning the edges back and gumming them to the back of the plate with varnish (stopping-out varnish answers well for this purpose).

You then draw your subject with a pencil on the paper, and on removing the paper you will remove at the same time, if only your pressure has been what it ought to have been, just so much of the ground as will expose the copper sufficiently to represent pencil-marks when bitten. The biting has to be done by stopping-out, and so you get the different degrees of blackness necessary to your effect. If afterwards the plate needs reinforcing anywhere, this can be done by grounding it in the ordinary manner and etching a little here and there with the point, only care must be taken to harmonise the different kinds of work, which might easily be dissonant.

I lay little stress upon this kind of etching, because although it is a positive process, and therefore so far superior in convenience to the old negative process of needle-etching, still it achieves nothing which cannot be equally well achieved in another way, namely by lithography. The etching needle has no rival on its own ground; what the etching needle can do, no other instrument in the world can do, or anything like it. But this process of soft ground etching, even when most successful, is not in any way better than lithography, whilst it cannot be so cheaply printed. I should say, therefore, that if the student prefers an etching of this kind to needle etching, he would do better to abandon that art altogether and take to lithography at once, because in that case lithography would probably reward him better.

CHAPTER VI.

Bracquemond's Pen Process.

M. BRACQUEMOND perfected, two or three years ago, a kind of etching with a common pen and ordinary ink, which had first been suggested to him by vague hints and traditions which had reached him.

According to this process, you begin by cleaning the plate very thoroughly first with turpentine and afterwards with whitening, after which you abstain from touching the surface of it with the fingers.

You then draw upon it with ordinary ink and a common steel pen, making in fact a free pen-drawing.

When you have done, you let the ink dry perfectly, and then ground and smoke the plate in the old-fashioned way (*see* "Old Process").

Then you immediately immerse the plate in water. After a quarter of an hour of immersion you rub it gently with a flannel. The ink having been softened by the water detaches both itself and the ground from the plate, and leaves the copper bare wherever it has been. You then immerse the plate in the bath, and bite it as usual.

This process, when skilfully followed, gives a very accurate and effective imitation of pen-drawing, just as the process described in Chapter V. imitates pencil-drawings. The plate may afterwards be worked up in the usual manner for delicate touches, as the pen lines are somewhat coarse.

My experience of this process is extremely limited, as I soon found a substitute for it, more agreeable to my own predilections, which will be described in the next chapter. The specimens with which Bracquemond himself has favoured me are enough to prove that in very skilful hands the process may be extremely effectual for the imitation of rather rude pen sketches, but not, I should think, for work in which it would be necessary to have very thin lines. As to paleness and blackness, they may of course be made as pale or as black as you like, because you have all the resources of biting at command, just as you have in ordinary point etching.

CHAPTER VII.

Hamerton's Brush Process.

THIS process is founded upon Bracquemond's pen process, but is more certain. The pigment used is thicker than any which can be used with a pen, and is easily destroyed in the acid bath. The essential peculiarity of this process is the employment of a pigment which the acid strongly attacks. The process therefore does not simply depend upon the solubility of ink in water, as Bracquemond's does, but upon the action of acid on an alkali.

1. CLEANING THE PLATE.

Clean the plate perfectly with whitening and turpentine. Remove the whitening at last by rubbing the plate well with bread. After this, do not touch the plate with your fingers.

2. THE PIGMENT.

Crush a soft pastel into fine powder and mix it, with a palette knife with a strong solution of white sugar. Add a solution of ox-gall about equal in quantity to half the sugar solution.

3. THE BRUSH.

Use a small fine-pointed sable-hair brush, and let the pigment be so mixed as to work rather freely, and draw a thin line on the copper with ease and precision.

4. THE DRAWING.

Use the point of the brush very much as if it were

a pen, depending mainly upon lines, but indulging yourself in a blot occasionally where a blot would be useful, just as a clever artist does in a pen sketch. If your plate has been properly cleaned, and your pigment properly mixed, you will be able to draw as easily as on a sheet of paper.

When you have done you still carefully refrain from touching the surface of the plate, or from letting anything else touch it. The pigment dries slowly. It does not much matter whether it is quite dry or not when you come to the next stage of the work.

5. THE GROUND.

Make a solution in ether of the ordinary etching ground described at page 1.

6. LAYING THE GROUND.

It is to be applied as collodion (*see* page 33). To expel the ether, heat gently over a spirit-lamp, holding the plate about twelve inches above the flame, and taking care that the ether in the ground is gradually expelled and does not catch fire.

This done, the ground will have become transparent, and lost the frosted appearance it had at first.

7. THE BATH.

Use Haden's bath (*see* page 26), and leave the plate in it a quarter of an hour without touching it. Then brush the surface of the plate very gently with a feather. This will disengage the pigment, and the ether varnish over it, leaving the lines exposed to the action of the acid. If the operation has been properly conducted from the beginning, all the lines will be clear, but the copper between them, even in the smallest squares or lozenges, will be perfectly protected.

HAMERTON'S BRUSH PROCESS. 25

You now leave the plate to bite according to the depth you require, stopping out when necessary, as in the old process.

The brush process, like Bracquemond's pen process, does not admit of very delicate lines, so the plate may be either finished in dry point or else completed by the addition of point-etching. In the latter case the artist will use a transparent ground.

The brush process is most useful for rich foregrounds, especially in rather large plates. The brush has one advantage over the etching needle, namely its capacity for obtaining accent by the enlargement of the line. This is often very convenient. For example, you may draw a blade of grass from point to root with a single stroke of the brush, but you could not do it with less than two strokes of the etching-needle. Again, with the brush, you may obtain many of the effects of the pen, especially its valuable power of blotting, which when rightly used is often most artistic.

During the progress of your work you may efface as much as you like, but it must be done with the scraper, not with water. With the same instrument you may *take out lights* exactly as in water-colour drawing.

Remember that if a blot is *too* wide, it will not print well. The ink would be taken out in the middle by the wiping of the printer's hand.

<small>The operations in the brush process are very delicate, and partial failure may be expected at first. If the ink does not take on the plate, you may roughen the copper very slightly by a short immersion in a weak nitric bath. Let the ether ground remain a night on the copper before you heat it, and be very cautious about the heating. I myself have not yet had time to acquire certainty of operation in the brush process, but feel sure that it may be acquired by care and observation.</small>

CHAPTER VIII.

Haden's Negative Process.

Mr. Seymour Haden was the first etcher to conceive the idea of executing a plate from beginning to end in the acid.

Having first discovered a slow and particularly safe mordant, not so disagreeable in odour as the old one, he placed his plate in the acid to begin with, and drew his subject in the acid.

1. The Mordant.

Hydrochloric acid . .	100 grammes.
Chlorate of potash . .	20 ,,
Water	880 ,,

The water is to be warmed and the chlorate of potash perfectly dissolved in it first, then the acid is to be added.

A word of warning is necessary here. The etcher is not to use the common muriatic acid of commerce, which disengages intolerable fumes and is of a deep yellow colour. I find that country druggists sometimes maintain that there is no other hydrochloric acid than that, and treat the applicant who asks for it disdainfully. The hydrochloric acid the etcher needs does not fume, and when mixed with water has but a slight odour.

2. Time of Biting.

When the weather is not very warm the lines intended to be darkest may be allowed to bite from five to seven hours, the palest one quarter. It is evident, therefore, that one has the time to execute a free etching in the bath, and put a considerable amount of work into it.

3. Principles of Work in the Acid.

You have merely to begin with the lines intended to be darkest, using a blunt point, and keeping them rather wide apart (according to Lalanne's rule), after that gradually proceeding towards the paler work, where you will use a sharper point, and make your lines closer.

If you calculate your time well, and do your work properly, your plate will be finished with a perfect gradation when you take it out of the bath, and you may print a proof of it at once.

4. The Tray.

The most convenient tray for working according to this process is a drawing-board of some very light wood, an inch and a half thick. In the middle of this a well is hollowed an inch deep, and three legs are adapted to it, exactly of the sort used by photographers for setting up a camera. By means of this arrangement a perfect level may be secured in any ground, and then the etcher will put his plate in the well. Of course a hand-rest is required, which may be a thin piece of deal or cedar just strong enough to bear the hand over the acid without yielding.

It is better to have only just acid enough to cover the plate, because if there is any considerable depth of it there is an inconvenience about the real position of the plate and its apparent position.

The etcher will feel some embarrassment at first from the necessity of marking only very dark lines in the earlier stages of his work, but he will overcome this with a little perseverance. The dark lines once established, will guide to the positions of the paler ones, and it will be found less difficult to draw on this principle than beginners usually imagine.

5. ADVANTAGES OF HADEN'S PROCESS.

First. *Perfect gradation in work.* All other systems of biting proceed by stages, usually two or three stages. This system of Mr. Haden's is one of unbroken gradation from the deepest biting to the palest.

Second. It saves the necessity for stopping-out, which was a cause of delay and difficulty in all passages of any intricacy, such as skies seen between the branches of trees, &c.

Third. It enables an experienced etcher to complete a plate at one sitting without being delayed by re-grounding, proof-taking, &c.

6. IMAGINARY DIFFICULTIES.

If you mention the process to any old-fashioned etcher he will laugh at you. He will also, most probably, look you in the face with an air of conscious superiority, as if he knew that you had stupidly forgotten something of which he was clearly conscious. Then he will say, "And what becomes of the needle?" This means that the needle will be dissolved by the acid.

Of course the point of the needle which is in the bath is constantly, though slowly, dissolving, but the action of the bath is merely to keep it sharp, and the money loss is so small as to be imperceptible, not exceeding sixpence a year.

An imaginary difficulty of this kind stops many people. The cost and inconvenience caused by the dissolution of the point in the acid do not equal the cost and inconvenience caused by the wearing away of the lead in pencil drawing, yet the old-fashioned etcher is stopped by the one, and, from habit, thinks nothing of the other.

Another difficulty, equally imaginary, is the notion that there is no certainty of procedure when you etch in the acid, that the result must be curiously unexpected, "due to chance," and so on. The fact is that as the acid bites very slowly and in the most regular manner, the weights of tone may be decided quite accurately beforehand by referring to a watch. There is no hurry whatever about the process, and if you are interrupted you have only to take your plate out of the bath and keep it out till your next sitting.

Some people say that a plate etched in the acid is bitten five or six times sooner than one etched out of the acid. This is a pure delusion, based on nervous fears. The simple truth is that the two are bitten in precisely the same length of time, if the acid in each case is of the same strength, and the temperature equal. You may increase the rapidity of biting on a portion of the plate about the size of a shilling by fixing the etching needle there, because the contact of the two metals in the acid establishes a galvanic battery, and copper flies off within a certain limited radius.

7. Real Objections to Haden's Process.

Mr. Haden's process is excellent for a master of the art, who has got accustomed to it, but is not suitable for beginners, or for timid practitioners, because it requires such certainty of hand, and such accurate calculation of the future value of the lines. Again, whilst the plate is in the bath, *the differences are always lessening.* For example, a line laid at the very beginning, and a line laid an hour afterwards, are, when the plate has been an hour and a half in the bath, of very different value, but as the plate remains longer and longer in the bath they are constantly approaching in value. This has to be continually taken into account, and it adds to the difficulty of the process.

Another real objection to Haden's process is that the mordant he uses *darkens* the copper as it bites, so that after a time it becomes difficult to see the lines that have been already etched. This may be temporarily overcome by resting the iron point for a few seconds on the plate in the part which you desire to see. The galvanic action above-mentioned will clear the lines, so that you will see them all plainly enough. But this is only temporary, they darken again when the iron is removed.

By using a weak nitric bath instead of Mr. Haden's, the difficulty is removed, and the lines remain light-coloured. The nitric bath, however, is not so safe as Mr. Haden's bath, I mean it is not so reliable as a mordant. For tranquil certainty of operation no bath that I have ever tried is equal to Mr. Haden's.

Finally, it is clear that with this process correction is out of the question. You cannot alter and amend unless when the plate ought to be finished you correct it by the tedious old processes. As the line is laid, so it must remain, hollowing itself deeper and deeper into the dissolving metal. This is a very serious objection in the case of almost all amateurs, and of many artists (not by any means the worst generally), who, though able to produce admirable works by correction and laborious care, have no natural talent for improvisation.

CHAPTER IX.

Hamerton's Negative Process.

The following negative process, which I used before discovering the positive one, may be recommended as avoiding some of the chief difficulties of other processes. It avoids stopping-out altogether, and there is considerable certainty about the result, as you may calculate your values of light and dark pretty accurately.

1. THE GROUND.

Make a clear solution of beeswax in turpentine, decanting it till no sediment of any kind remains. The solution should be perfectly fluid, and of a bright clear yellow colour.

To this solution add one-sixth of its volume of japan varnish, but you must vary the quantity of varnish according to the heat of the weather. If there is too much of it, the ground will be hard and brittle; if there is too little, the ground will not be strong enough to take smoke with safety.

2. APPLICATION OF THE GROUND.

First clean the plate with engraver's emery paper, and then plunge it in a Haden's bath till it darkens all over. This change of colour assures you that there is no grease, and it assists the adherence of the ground. The slight roughening is easily removed afterwards.

Then pour the ground on the plate as the photographers pour collodion, and let it dry for twelve hours. After that, apply a second coat of the ground in the same manner, and smoke the second coat immediately without waiting for it to dry. The result is a ground perfectly even and smooth, so that it reflects everything like a mirror, and so equally sound that you may etch all over it with equal safety.

It is the most satisfactory ground I have ever tried; but it hardens afterwards by time, and ought therefore to be used within a few days after it is laid.

It is not absolutely necessary to allow the first coat to dry slowly. If you are in haste to use the plate you may expel what is volatile in the turpentine by passing the flame of a spirit lamp under the plate till the ground becomes quite transparent; then let it cool, and as soon as the plate is cold pour the second coat over it and smoke immediately. If these operations have been properly performed, you will have a quite perfect ground.

3. REASON FOR THE APPLICATION OF TWO COATS.

Grounds which are applied in a fluid state are necessarily very thin; and if you smoke a single coat sufficiently to make it really black you introduce a quantity of lamp black into the ground, which alters its chemical constitution so that it becomes weak, does not adhere well, and though it may seem right when you are working with the point, will detach itself in the acid bath. By applying two coats and smoking rapidly you ensure adherence, because the first coat is not altogether penetrated by the smoke, and it is this first coat which resists the acid, whereas the second retains the lamp-black.

4. WHEN THE GROUND IS TOO HARD.

You may find the ground too hard for a blunt point when it is still in good condition for a sharper point; but if it is too hard for a sharp point, you may still make it serve by gently heating the plate on a warm lithographic stone, and keeping it there whilst you work. Increase, when the ground is hard, the proportion of the wax solution.

5. DRAWING AND BITING.

Draw all the dark parts first, then plunge the plate in the bath for one half the total time of biting, whichever bath you use. For instance, if it were a Haden's bath, in winter the total time would be six hours, so your first biting would be for three hours; a Haden's bath in hot weather would require four hours, so your first biting would be for two hours; a nitric bath in temperate weather would be for half-an-hour, so your first biting would be fifteen minutes.

Then take your plate out, dry it with blotting paper, and draw the *next darkest* lines wherever they are wanted. Immerse the plate for one-fourth of the total time.

Take it out again, add the paler tones, but not the palest. Immerse for one-eighth of the total time.

Finally, draw all the palest work in the plate. Immerse for one-eighth of the total time.

If the reader is reading carelessly (as I am afraid most readers do, especially reviewers) it will seem to him that the third and fourth bitings are for equal lengths, being each set down for one-eighth of the time. However, as the third biting is still going forward with the fourth, it is really of double duration, and the account, at last, stands thus:—

The darkest lines have bitten the whole time.
The darker lines have bitten half the time.
The paler lines have bitten a quarter of the time.
The palest lines have bitten one-eighth of the time.

Add to this a little retouching with the dry point, and the plate is finished.

6. A Standard for Biting.

Every etcher ought to etch a standard plate with the various depths of shading obtained by these different bitings. By reference to this, he will be able to ascertain beforehand the effect of what he is doing.

It is well in this process to follow somewhat rigidly Lalanne's doctrine about lines, and to use four points for the four sittings, the bluntest first, the sharpest last.

CHAPTER X.

Hamerton's Positive Process.

1. Purpose of a Positive Process.

By my positive process the artist, whilst he is etching, sees his work in black upon a white ground, as distinctly as if he were drawing with a lead pencil on white paper, instead of seeing it in copper on a black ground.

The old negative process is not only objectionable because it is *negative*, but also because the lines are *brilliant*, which causes them to appear more rich and numerous than they really are.

A star seen by the naked eye appears very much larger than the same star seen through a telescope, although the telescope magnifies it many times. The reason for this is, that the glittering rays about the star which dazzle the naked eye are shorn away by the telescope.

In the same way the lines of glittering copper in the old system of etching appear richer and more abundant than they really are, because of their deceptive glitter.

They deceive also in another way. Those which run at right angles to the rays of light appear brighter and more numerous than those which are parallel with the rays.

The consequence of these deceptions is, that it needs a vast experience to know accurately the state of a plate before you see a proof of it, and even the most experienced etchers are liable to frequent deceptions.

In nine cases out of ten a plate is much poorer than it looks, and requires a considerable amount of after labour to bring it up to the degree of richness which the etcher believes himself to have already attained.

In a positive process, on the other hand, when the lines do not glitter but show as dull darks on white, there is no deception of this kind.

It is unnecessary to add that a positive process which shows those lines dark that are to appear dark in the printing, is plainer than a negative process in which every dark line is represented by a light one. The difference is, that in the negative processes the artist *calculates* what he is doing, whereas in the positive process he *sees* what he is doing.

2. THE SILVERING OF THE PLATE.

As a copper plate, however well polished, is still rather dark in colour, I silver it to make it lighter.

The most convenient way of silvering a plate is to use *crême d'argent* (a cyanide of silver), or silvering powder.

You simply mix a little of the powder with water and put it on a clean rag, and rub your plate with it. The plate must be well cleaned previously. Rub it gently; and your plate will be properly silvered.

3. TO MAKE THE SILVER OF A DEAD WHITE.

Roughen the surface of the copper slightly before silvering with fine emery paper, letting the lines run in the direction which will be from right to left, or from left to right, whilst you are at work. This catches the light on the surface of the plate, and makes it white.

The white ground, in drying, deadens the silver still farther.

4. THE WHITE GROUND.

Dissolve white wax in ether, making what chemists call a saturated solution. Let it settle a few days. There will be a clear part, and a milky part, below it. The clear solution is what you want, because the milky part is not really a solution, but a suspension of undissolved particles, many of which are perfectly insoluble in ether, when, as most commonly happens, the white wax has been adulterated with starch or other white powder. In fact, by making the solution in ether, you at the same time ensure the purification of the wax, which is a great thing in itself. Your clear solution will be white wax, in as pure a state as can be, when the ether has evaporated.

5. APPLYING THE GROUND.

Pour the solution in the same way as described at page 33 on the silvered side till it makes a pool reaching to the edges of the plate. Then incline the plate gently, yet firmly, and rather quickly, so that the solution may run first to one corner and then to another, till finally, you pour all the superfluous solution back into the bottle. In finishing, you should move the plate rapidly, so that first a long side of the plate may be vertical and then a short one.

Let the ground remain three days to dry. Then apply a second coat of wax in the same manner. Let the second coat remain four days before you make use of the plate. Lean the plate against a wall in a quiet room where nobody goes, its face to the wall, so that it may not catch dust.

If you accelerate the drying by the heat of a spirit-lamp, you obtain transparence but lose the dead white, which is desirable.

6. THE BACK AND EDGES OF THE PLATE.

Paint the back and edges of the plate with stopping out varnish, to protect them.

7. THE BATH.

It is essential to use Haden's bath, because it gives a dark line. The nitric bath gives a light-coloured line, and is therefore useless for our purpose.

The Haden bath is composed as follows:—Chlorate of potash 20 grammes, hydrochloric acid 100 gr., water 880 gr. If you have not French weights, the same proportion may easily be preserved in English ones. First warm the water and dissolve the chlorate of potash in it; then add the acid. Mind that your hydrochloric acid is pure (*see* p. 26).

8. THE SKETCH.

You may trace your subject by rubbing a little pastel behind a piece of paper on which you sketch it.

Or you may sketch it directly, on the white ground with the point of a small sable-hair brush, charged with a little water-colour.

In either case use some pale but decided colour that cannot prevent you from seeing the etched lines, bright red, or yellow, for example.

Enough of it will remain visible in the bath for an indication.

9. THE PLATE TO BE ETCHED IN THE BATH.

The plate must be etched in the bath *according to Mr. Haden's process*, otherwise the lines would not darken sufficiently (*see* p. 26).

10. The Drawing-Board.

The drawing-board to be used is the same as recommended for Haden's negative process at page 27.

Do not have the well for the porcelain tray cut in the middle of the board, but towards the top of it, thus: as it is much more convenient. In etching an upright subject with the same board, have the broad margin to your right hand.

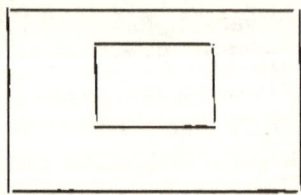

Let the board be entirely japanned with several coats of japan, say six coats. The dark colour of this makes the plate look whiter, and the japan protects the wood efficaciously against the acid.

You may imagine that there is no use in having the well so deep, as the bath is only just to cover the plate; but if your bath is too shallow, the acid by capillary attraction will get into the small space between your hand-rest and the board and very soon flood the whole board, and spoil your sleeve. Any flat piece of thin wood will do for a hand-rest (*see* Haden's negative process, page 27).

For etching from nature I prefer a wooden or gutta-percha tray to the drawing-board, because it is much lighter and smaller.

11. To fix the Plate in the Bath.

Lay it exactly where you wish it to be, and take four balls of modelling wax about the size of a marble. Press each of them strongly with the thumb, so that the wax may cover a corner of the plate and spread upon the the tray or drawing-board. The plate will then adhere firmly and travel safely.

12. THE BLACKENING OF THE LINE.

If the bath is in a right condition the line will blacken the instant you draw it, but it will not do so in a perfectly new bath.* Hence, before beginning to work, dissolve a small bit of copper in the bath. I also add a bit of zinc.

13. THE ENLARGEMENT OF THE LINE.

The wax ground is quite safe, but it permits the lines to enlarge slowly. There is consequently a perfect gradation in thickness from the earliest lines to the latest, as the time of exposure diminishes. This is most fortunate, being exactly what the etcher needs, and in strict accordance with Lalanne's doctrine about lines.

14. THE NEEDLE TO BE USED IN THE POSITIVE PROCESS.

In consequence of the enlargement of the line we dispense with a variety of blunt and sharper points in this process, using one point only, a rather strong sewing-needle inserted in a holder. It should always be sharp enough to scratch well through the silver, that the copper may be attacked by the mordant at once, without which the line would not blacken instantaneously.

15. HOW TO DEAL WITH A SKETCH CONTAINING LESS THAN FIVE HOURS WORK.

You require five hours for the biting of the darkest lines, consequently the plate *must* remain in the bath

---

* Etchers who will not pay attention to this will incur complete disappointment, as with a new bath the positive process is not possible.

five hours. If you wish to give only two hours work, you must so distribute them over a space of five hours that the lines you draw may reach the degree of value in light and shade which you desire. In the intervals you may carry forward another plate in the same way.

16. HOW TO DEAL WITH A PLATE THAT REQUIRES SEVERAL SITTINGS.

From the account just given of the positive process, the reader may see how a single-sitting plate may be carried through successfully (as in the Haden process), but he may not see at once how to deal with a plate that requires several sittings.

Suppose the case of an elaborate plate requiring five sittings of six hours each.

Begin at first with a selection of the work *over the whole plate*, amounting to one-fifth of the total labour to be given. Then clean the plate and ground it afresh. In the second sitting you will also go gradually over the whole plate in the same manner, adding work to that which already exists. So in the remaining sittings. You cannot, whilst working in the acid, do the whole of the foreground in one sitting, and the whole of the distance in another, on account of the operation of the acid, but you must so time your different sittings as to work always at the same hour on tones intended to be of the same depth. There is no difficulty or inconvenience about this when you get accustomed to it.

12. TO CORRECT BY EFFACING WORK.

Proceed at first exactly as if there were no silver on the plate, boldly using scraper, charcoal, &c., and re-silver, &c., afterwards before re-touching, if re-touching is required.

13. CLEANING PLATES, &c.

Turpentine is usually employed for this purpose, but in giving an account of my own process, I may as well add that I find schist-oil a much better cleanser than turpentine. It leaves the hands, too, in a more agreeable condition, for everything except the smell, which may be got rid of by using plenty of scented soap. Petroleum is also much better than turpentine. Both schist-oil and petroleum remove Japan varnish very rapidly, whereas turpentine dissolves it slowly. Since using schist-oil, I find it possible to combine the pursuit of etching with decent-looking hands, which I never could manage with turpentine.*

---

* I discovered the positive process during the winter of 1870-71, but did not perfect it until the spring, so that I have not yet had time to acquire any great facility in it. However, my work this summer (1871) has satisfied me that the process itself may be relied upon, although it will need more practice than I have yet had time to give, to develop all its capabilities.

CHAPTER XI.

Of the Etching-needle or Point.

Mr. HADEN'S theory about the point is that it should be heavy, in order that the hand may not have to trouble itself much about pressure, but remain free to direct, simply, whilst the weight of the instrument itself penetrates the ground. He therefore uses a bar of steel sharpened at both ends, in shape something like a cigar or a stump. The ideal Haden point would be of gold, as the heaviest of metals, and the one which resists acid best.

My points are made in a single piece of soft iron for etching, not steel, that reserved for dry point only is of steel. They are exactly shaped like a lead-pencil sharpened to a fine point. I use a set of five,* one for dry-point work of steel, sharpened specially for dry point, and four others of iron, sharpened to different degrees of sharpness; No. 1 being very blunt indeed, for thick lines, and No. 4 pretty sharp. In addition to these, for the closest work of all, I use a common sewing-needle, fastened in a brass holder. My holder is merely a mathematical steel pen, which holds the needle between its two halves, and I drop sealing-wax between them to fix it.

When the etching-needle is all in one piece it is more certain to be firm, but the point should be sharpened to a very acute angle, or else the thickness of the iron itself will often prevent the artist from seeing what he is doing.

* For negative etching in my positive process I use one point only, a sewing-needle fixed in a holder.

CHAPTER XII.

The Dry Point.

WHAT etchers call the Dry Point is merely an ordinary etching-needle (of steel), sharpened in a peculiar manner, and used without either etching-ground, or acid-bath, on the bare copper.

The difference between etchers' Dry Point and engravers' Dry Point is, that the etchers look to the bur for their effect, whilst the engravers look to the line without the bur.

The bur is a ridge of copper, which is raised by the point in passing, just as when you make a furrow with a plough, the earth that you push up makes a ridge above the level of the ground. The bur in printing catches the printing-ink in a peculiar way, by protecting a certain margin of smooth copper against the operation of the printer's hand when he wipes the plate. The ink remains on this smooth copper, but passes away from the bur with a delicate gradation which gives a certain softness to the line.

The more perpendicular the dry point is whilst you are at work, the less bur you will have, the more you incline the instrument to your right, the more bur you will have, if the pressure in both cases is equal.

The ideal of dry-point work for an etcher is so to calculate his pressure that when the line is done it shall not be necessary to remove the bur at all, because he ought to produce his results with, and by, the bur; but dry point is often used for shades in ordinary etched plates, to which it gives a certain delicate finish. In this case all the bur is removed. In pure dry-point work it is often necessary to remove a part of the bur, and the way to do that is to use the scraper *at right angles to the line*, consequently, if a cross-hatching has to be reduced by the scraper it is better to draw first the lines that run in one direction, and scrape them, and afterwards those that run in another, and scrape *them*. Always keep your scraper very sharp, if not, it will scratch the copper.

Dry point has one very great advantage over ordinary etching, it is a positive process. The artist may easily see what he is doing by rubbing a mixture of tallow and lamp-black over the plate, and removing what is superfluous with a rag. That which remains is sufficient to produce exactly the effect which the plate will produce in the printing, with the difference that the copper is not of the same tint as the paper, so that the etching does not look so brilliant as it will on the paper.

Formerly, dry points could not be printed beyond very small editions (from fifty to a hundred copies) but since the invention of steeling (protecting the copper by means of an infinitesimally thin coat of steel applied by galvanism) a dry point will yield larger editions than an etching would formerly. Hence the art will probably become more general.

In comparing the practice of this art with etching, the student will perceive that he has much less liberty in dry-point, but this is partially compensated by the resources of the art in the way of rich velvety effects. However, the practice of it is a separate study from etching, and it would not be treated of in works on etching if etchers did not habitually resort to it to finish or correct their plates.

CHAPTER XIII.

To Efface Faulty Passages.

WHENEVER you have a bit of irremediably bad work in an etching you may efface it entirely.

The most rapid way is to use sand-papers of different degrees of coarseness, the coarsest first, and then the scraper, and, finally, willow charcoal with olive oil. The charcoal will leave the surface in a fit state to etch upon.

This scraping and rubbing hollows the surface of the copper, and if it hollows it too much the printing will not be quite satisfactory in that part of the plate. In that case you have nothing to do but mark the spot on the back of the plate with a pair of callipers, then lay the plate on its face upon a block of polished steel, and give it two or three blows with a hammer (mind that the hammer is rounded so as not to indent the copper).

The only objection to this way of effacing is the time it takes. If you have a trustworthy coppersmith in your neighbourhood, you may first show him what has to be done, and then send your coppers to him when a part requires effacing, but you cannot trust engraved plates in the hands of most workmen, as they are too careless and always scratch them. The professional copper-planers for engravers do this work as a part of their business, and may be trusted.

CHAPTER XIV.

To Reduce a Passage that is Overbitten.

USE willow-charcoal with olive oil, and nothing else, as scrapers and sand-paper injure the edges of the line, whereas willow-charcoal does not injure their quality at all, but merely reduces the copper.

In consequence of the facility with which an over-bitten passage may be reduced, it is always better to bite too much than too little. I have shown elsewhere that re-biting is in great part illusory. The lines which are deep already are deepened still farther, those which are shallow are protected by the ground. But there is no corresponding difficulty in reducing an over-bitten passage, because all the lines are reduced equally. It is sometimes necessary, however, to efface pale lines altogether, in order to reduce deep ones sufficiently. In that case, the pale lines may be etched over again.

CHAPTER XV.

Etching from Nature.

ETCHING is the only kind of engraving which can be conveniently done directly from nature. Some of the best modern etchers work from nature habitually.

The necessary preparations are simple enough. On an excursion of several days the plates may be ready grounded and carried in a grooved box such as photographers use for their glasses. Or if you are only going out to etch a single plate you may carry it in a wooden portfolio made of two light boards with a frame between them to keep them from touching. The plate is easily fastened to one of these boards by two small screws. There is no necessity to bore holes in the plate (which would spoil the proofs), it may be fastened quite firmly to the board by the heads of the screws only.* If you use the old negative process these preparations are sufficient; if you employ Haden's process or mine (etching in the acid negatively or positively), you will need the drawing board with the well (*see* page 40), and may carry your plate in a grooved box.† You must have a little Japan or stopping out varnish with you to re-varnish the edges

---

* A simple tray is lighter than a drawing-board, and you may fix your plate firmly in its place before starting by pressing lumps of modelling wax upon its four corners and spreading the wax a little on the wood.

† The simplest and most convenient way of carrying *a pair* of negative plates, ready prepared, is this. Place a ball of modelling wax the size of a pea on each corner of the plate, upon the grounded

E

before you put the plate in the bath, as they will have been exposed by friction in the grooves. You need not burden yourself with the mordant already made. It is enough to have a little case of two stoppered bottles, one for the hydrochloric acid and another for chlorate of potash. You can get water elsewhere.

In etching from nature, always make it a rule to choose the kind of subjects best adapted to the art, and to yourself. Remember that for vegetation in all its forms etching is eminently adapted, and also for the picturesque in buildings or in animals and figures. On the other hand the art is not so well suited for those things in nature which require for their interpretation the accurate management of very delicate tones. If your eye is true, and well-educated, you will be able to hit the delicate relations of tone in distant mountain scenery, for example, with much accuracy in water-colour and in a very short time, but with exactly the same artistic ability you will find it monstrously difficult in etching. On the other hand, you may etch a rich weedy foreground, a group of picturesque cottages, a group of trees, or any material of that kind, in the most satisfactory manner if you are naturally fitted for the art, and have mastered it. So in figures you will find it supremely difficult to

side, lay the other plate so that its four corners may rest upon the four balls of wax and the two plates be face to face. Then press the plates together till the balls of wax are flattened to the shape of cheeses. The plates will now stick together firmly enough, but without touching each other, and they will protect each other against everything else. Slip them into a bag of strong cloth made to fit them like a glove, and you may carry them in your pocket as easily as a pocket-book. This dispenses with boards and boxes which are unnecessary.

give the modelling of a naked figure because that depends upon *tones*, but you will find the art perfectly well adapted to render a beggar's tattered dress, or the wrinkled face of an old woman, because truth here may be effectively expressed by lines.

In a word, wherever the line, as such, has great expressional value, etching triumphs easily, but where nothing can be done without very accurate tonality, the technical difficulties are so great that it requires years of labour given to this especial art to overcome them.

In working from nature remember that shading may be made to express a great deal about form when it is used ingeniously, quite independently of what is expressed by the degree of light or dark it gives. The direction of shading is often explanatory of surface. For instance, if in shading a thatched roof you make your lines go in the same direction as the blades of straw, they will explain a good deal about the nature of the roof, and if you shade moss with dots instead of lines you will suggest the nature of moss, because in nature it is always dotted. There are a thousand things of this kind which you will find out for yourself in working with the view of making your lines always as explanatory as you possibly can. One tree has its bark strongly marked by longitudinal divisions, you may take advantage of these, and make them both give darks to your etching and an explanation of the nature of the tree. Or if, as in the birch, the bark strips of horizontally, you may explain this fact by the direction of your shading.

The great etchers, in the course of their practice, have authorised a sort of conventional language of the art which every etcher ought to learn; for it is based on rational principles, like all that is good in the fine arts. For example, if you were etching a sky you would naturally use horizontal and not perpendicular lines. Why? There are no lines of either kind in nature. The great etchers, however, have always used horizontal lines for skies, and we continue the tradition of this practice, because we can obtain a gradation so much more easily across many lines than in the direction of one line. It is true that in every sky there are two gradations, one from the horizon to the zenith, and the other from right to left, or from left to right, but the first is by far the stronger and more obvious of the two, and therefore the best etchers have so arranged their lines as to accomplish that gradation the more easily.

There is not space, in a little handbook, to follow out a subject of this kind in detail, but two pieces of advice may be given which, if properly followed, will make the student's career a safe one in this respect. The first is to make your lines as much as possible *serve two purposes at the same time*, namely that of producing darks where darks are needed in your plan of chiaroscuro, and that of explaining the nature of the thing you are drawing. The second piece of advice is, when you have recourse to conventional interpretation, always to choose, whenever you possibly can, those conventionalisms which have been already used by great etchers in past times, because they already constitute a sort of language which is understood by all who have studied the art. Have no fear that by doing this your originality need be sacrificed. Do not authors of books use words which are conventional signs, and which have been in use for centuries, and yet display their originality, when they have any, nevertheless? It is wiser to use a sign that will be understood by the class to which you address yourself than one which will have to be learned like a foreign word. Study some really genuine etcher, Rembrandt, or Claude, or Vandyke,* and learn his language, in which afterwards you may express your own ideas with such modifications as may be necessary.

Remember, in working from nature, that much of the peculiar value of a fine etching, much that distinguishes it from an engraving by the burin, is its artistic heat and vivacity. A *cold* etching is a bad etching. Hence, when you work from nature, never attempt anything that does not really cause you some kind of strong artistic emotion, and work only so long as the emotion lasts. If your impression has been powerful, and you are able to render a powerful impression rapidly, you will most likely produce *living* work; but if you are only half-interested, and work in a quiet professional way to do the day's labour, without caring much about the subject, or much enjoying the art, then the work will be dead work and not of the least value. The spirit of laborious painters and engravers who give infinite time and trouble to the elaboration of one effect is a good spirit in their arts, which produce their results by patient accumulation of steadily and scientifically directed labour, but the state of mind in which

* The portraits before the formal engraver-like backgrounds were added.

an artist etches best is that in which he ardently and passionately desires to set down a thought whilst it is yet most fresh and most vivid. Mr. Haden goes so far as to say that an etching ought to be done in a single sitting. This is not always possible, but it is wise to give only so many sittings as we can go through without losing the first impression. Or, you may give one sitting direct from nature, and finish afterwards in the house to get the work better together, always in view of the impression you received from nature. In some respects this plan is better than going to nature several times, because if you see the subject on different days, when the effects are different, and you yourself are in a different temper, there will very likely come a sort of confusion over your mind, not as to the *things* you saw (the houses, trees, or what not), but as to the unity of impression, which depends quite as much upon the temporary effect, and the temporary state of your own mind (even upon the book you have been reading in the morning, or the letter you have received) as upon the material things before you.

CHAPTER XVI.

Etchings to be Studied.

I HAVE not space to give here anything like a critical account of the best etchers, and have already given it elsewhere, but a few words as to the study of examples may not be out of place, or unnecessary.

The more study you give to Rembrandt's work, the better your method is likely to become. No man ever loved the art of etching more, or understood it better. There are many kinds of imperfections in his plates, and it would be easy for any moderately accomplished critic to point them out, but in almost every instance they are perfect models of technical execution, if you take into consideration the time Rembrandt intended to give to each. The 'Christ Healing the Sick,' for various degrees of finish skilfully united in the same plate, the 'Descent from the Cross by Torchlight,' and the 'Three Crosses,' for masterly rapid work in naked line, and the 'Death of the Virgin' for grandeur of method everywhere, and perfect use of means, are the most notable amongst the sacred subjects. Of the "allegories and fancies," the 'Youth surprised by Death' is the most delicate and refined in manner. A good many of the beggars are worth careful study, especially the one with the large belly. Nearly all the portraits are fine, and one of the best pleasures of an etcher is to look over any fine set of impressions of them. The early portrait of his mother, done at the age of twenty-two, is a model of right workmanship on a small scale, and so are old Haaring, Janus Lutma, and the nameless man with the silvery beard and the fur cap on a larger.

Amongst the landscapes take the 'View of Omval' as a model of work with the etching-needle, and the 'Landscape with the three Cottages' as a model of work with the dry point. Rembrandt's knowledge of landscape was inferior to that possessed by modern landscape painters (no branch of art has advanced so much *scientifically*, during this century, as landscape), but his technical execution, as an etcher, is better than modern execution usually is.*

Ostade's execution was good and sound in its way, but quite simple, lacking the great *resources* of Rembrandt's. His fame depends more upon his truth to peasant life and his clever composition. Paul Potter drew beautifully with the point, but does not seem ever to have understood sketching, and thoroughly good intelligent sketching is the foundation of great etching. Study the 'Bull' and the three etchings of Horses.

Study everything of Vandyke's with scrupulous care. You may learn a good deal in landscape etching from Waterloo and Weirotter. Weirotter attained remarkable truth of tonality, which is not common, and he attained it by quite simple means.

* If the reader has not access to original etchings by Rembrandt he is warned not to trust much to the photographs from them. No etching in which the resources of the art are called into play can possibly be photographed. The photographs are nothing but reminders for students who know the originals. Study Flameng's small and precious copies in Charles Blanc's catalogue rather.

Some of Canaletti's etchings are worth studying. The best of them is 'La Torre di Malghera,' chiefly to be recommended for general luminousness and for the clever execution of the buildings.

Amongst Frenchmen Claude is the best landscape etcher of past days, and Lalanne the best of the present day. Claude had a wonderful tenderness in handling, and got extraordinarily delicate tones, very perfect in gradation. The 'Herdsman' and the 'Sunset' are the two most perfect of Claude's plates. Boissieu was very clever, too, in getting delicate and accurate tones, and in imitating objects; follow him in his truth of tone, but not in his deceptive imitation. Méryon's etchings of architecture are the best examples in the world of the treatment of architecture, which is not ruinous, in artistic etching. The skill with which he could draw one clear unhesitating line, full of life from beginning to end, and yet as accurate as was compatible with the expression of artistic feeling, has never been equalled in the art. He used to etch from nature standing, and holding the plate in his left hand, which held at the same time a small mirror to reverse the subject.* Then he drew the lines on his plate, quite steadily and firmly, yet without erring either on the side of carelessness of form or forgetfulness of feeling. Feats of this kind, which are performed by Méryon without any idea of display, and were known only to one or two artists

---

* In etching from nature, if you wish the proofs of you plate to appear topographically true, you must of course use the mirror to counteract the reversing in the printing.

who had seen him at work by accident, are as astonishing as the feats of Paganini on the violin.

Lalanne is an etcher of uncommon ability technically, and of the most graceful and elegant taste. The 'Vue prise du Pont St. Michel' is on the whole, I think, the most perfect of all his works, the kind and quantity of labour given being everywhere settled beforehand with such perfect judgment. There is not a line too much, and the drawing is neither too rigid nor too free. No one but a most accomplished artist could etch such a work as this, because drawing of this kind must come right at once, or the failure is evident.

Jules Jacquemart, having devoted the whole of his time to etching, and being besides a man of the most consummate natural ability, has brought the art to a degree of imitative perfection which it never before attained. His works combine the accuracy and certainty of the most accomplished modern engraving, with the artistic liberty of the true etchers. All those things which the ignorant affirm to be impossible in etching, Jacquemart *does*, and does triumphantly well, every day of his life. You may therefore go to his works as proofs of what can be done in the art, and you will derive from them this lesson, that whenever you fail the fault lies in your own unskilfulness, and not in any defect of the process. On the other hand, you need not hope ever to rival Jacquemart on his own ground unless you give the whole of your time to the art, and are an uncommonly clever artist to begin with. To any one who did not give his *whole* time to etching, whether painter or not, such work as Jacquemart's is every bit as impossible as Robinson's engraving with the burin. Even Rembrandt himself could not have approached it on its own ground. It will do you good to study it, however, because you will hear much nonsense to the effect that etching cannot do this thing and cannot do that, which a knowledge of Jacquemart's work will enable you to estimate at its true value.

Charles Jacque is well worth studying too, and is a real *master*, knowing the art better than any other living painter; but since he has made experiments in different directions, most of them successful experiments, it is necessary to know a good deal about his works to form a correct general idea of him. Study rather his interpretative work, which looks somewhat rough, than his imitative work, which looks highly "finished."

Appian is one of the sweetest and best of living etchers, artistic and sensitive in a very high degree, and able to reach remarkable truth of tone. He is a delightful painter, and carries more of his painting into his etching than artists generally do. The unity, breadth and keeping of his execution are beyond praise.

Jongkind is an honest and observant etcher, with a strong natural faculty of a peculiar kind. All artists who are themselves able to make good rapid memoranda from nature appreciate Jongkind's etchings, which are nothing but a landscape painter's memoranda of impressions (done in about a quarter of an hour); but these etchings usually give intense offence to people who are not accustomed to the rough jottings by which artists set down their ideas. If they interest and affect you, making you feel as if you had been on the spot with Jongkind whilst he was sketching, and shared his impression, then you may learn a good deal from them; but if they offend you pass them by, and try not to think that all the eminent artists who like them are fools or idiots, their quality is not *vérité*, which they have not, but *vraisemblance*, which they have in the supreme degree.

Lastly, amongst modern Frenchmen, let me recommend Veyrassat, who is one of the very best of them all. There *can* be nothing better of that kind than his little etchings of horses. The perfect taste of the execution, the perfectly artistic manner, in which everything is given up to the right point and never beyond it, the simplicity of purpose, the absence of affectation, the absence of all thought of displaying the great stores of knowledge, without which work of this kind would not be possible to any one, are as admirable as, unfortunately, they are rare. The student will do well, however, to remember that work of this kind is in a high degree deceptive. It looks as simple and natural as an egg or a gooseberry, yet you can no more make it than you can make eggs and gooseberries, only you fancy you can, because it is a human product.

Of Englishmen Turner was a magnificent etcher in pure line, but his work is not so instructive as it might have been, because he looked to an after-process of mezzotint to complete the effect. Wilkie was a very excellent etcher, though he did not etch much. His plate of 'the Pope examining a Censer' is one of the most masterly plates in existence.

Amongst living men Whistler may be cited as an etcher of rare quality in one important respect, the management of line, but his etchings owe much of the strange charm which they possess to a Chinese disdain of tonic values, and to a wayward caprice, loving detail here and scorning it there, which, being strictly personal, can only be of use as an example in one sense, that it shows how valuable in the art is a genuine personal feeling. Whistler is an admirably delicate draughtsman when he likes; there are passages in his etchings which are as striking in their way as feats of execution, as the most wonderful passages of Meryon.

Mr. Haden, an eminent London surgeon, is of all living English etchers the one who has been most faithful to the principles of the art. Though an amateur, he is really also an artist, and a master-artist. He is a pupil of Rembrandt, and having allied much of what was best in Rembrandt's very fine and genuine technical manner to the modern knowledge of landscape, has produced work of quite a surprising quality. The excellence of it may be accounted for partly by the fact that Mr. Haden had always been in the habit of using drawing as an auxiliary in the study of anatomy, and that when he took to etching he was obliged to abandon the exercise of his profession for years in order to recruit his health, these years being employed chiefly in this particular art. The student cannot have a better model than Haden with reference to the technical use of line; but a student who attempted to produce, out of a spirit of mere imitation, anything resembling what Haden did in hours of strong and genuine feeling would probably fail ridiculously. There is much in Haden's work which it would not do to set as a model before boys any more than you would give them some strongly individual autograph to copy if they were learning to write, but his scribblings and scrawlings and scratchings are always right where he puts them, right for him, and in their right place.

The other English etchers are not generally to be recommended as examples of the most genuine work in the art, because, for the most part, they have set themselves to get painters' results or engravers' results rather than the special qualities of etching. For example, it is clear that the real teachers of Creswick were not the great etchers but the modern vignette engravers, and it is clear that the real aim of Samuel Palmer and Hook is to get as much as possible of the effect of their own pictures in water or oil. In these aims the modern English etchers have often succeeded very admirably indeed. Creswick's plates were charming; of Samuel Palmer's I know not how to say things beautiful enough to do justice to their beauty, so tender and full of feeling are they, and rich with such affluence of thought. Hook can paint with the point very exquisitely. (See his wonderful plate of 'The Egg Gatherer.') Frederick Tayler, as in the hunting scene in the 'Songs of Shakespeare,' ("What shall he have who killed the deer?"), pushes the craft of modern etching to its utmost possible limit.

But although these etchers, and others of the same school, have produced works which we cannot help admiring in their way, it is better not to imitate them, because they have led the art out of its natural and peculiar path. It is useless to employ an etching needle if we are not to avail ourselves of its superiorities. Etching is, like violin playing, capable of imitating other arts, and as a matter of curiosity it is interesting to see an etching which is like an engraving, and another which is like a mezzotint, and a third which is almost like a painting; just as it is amusing to hear a clever violinist imitate a hurdy-gurdy, or a flute, or a canary bird. But if we heard nothing else but these imitations we might be inclined to say, "Well, this is really very wonderful, but now, suppose the violinist were to imitate a violin?" As the violin is the great expressional instrument in music, so is the etching-needle the great expressional instrument in engraving, and to abandon its superiorities in order to aim at the qualities of other arts, is unwise, because the loss is greater than the gain. For example, although the etchings of Creswick were very pretty, the vignettes which the engravers made from Creswick's drawings were prettier still, and strictly in the same kind. And although Samuel Palmer's work is delightful, the delightfulness of it might be preserved in mezzotint. But that which constitutes the especial supremacy of etching, the accent of the free line, was in each of these cases, and has been by nearly all living English and German etchers, sacrificed as a violinist sacrifices the qualities of bowing when he imitates a guitar.

CHAPTER XVII.

The Training of an Etcher.

WITH few exceptions, etchers of high rank have hitherto been distinguished painters, to begin with. Still it is clear that although an etcher ought to know the effect of colour in black and white, he need not be a colourist. Again, as the etching-needle is a very different instrument from the brush, it does not seem absolutely necessary that an etcher should be able to use the brush in order to master the needle. What is absolutely essential is that he should be an artist before he uses the needle, that he should have studied drawing, and light and shade, and composition, in some other art, either with the brush or the crayon or the pencil, in water-colour, oil, chalk, charcoal, or anything out of itself.

But why, to learn etching, is etching itself the art most to be excluded?

Because, in etching, there is no immediate comparison possible between the model you are studying and the line you are making, so that study from nature is not so beneficial in etching as in other arts. Even in my positive process the *full* effect of what you do is not visible at once, as it is in pen-drawing, for example. To study beneficially, you ought to use some process which allows of incessant comparison.

Pen-drawing is very good, but it should be pen-drawing of a comprehensive kind, not mere outline only, but taking account of everything, including effect, and always on pure principles of *sketching*, however far the sketch may be carried. If you cannot sketch you cannot etch. And let me observe that the vulgar notion about the facility of sketching is a delusion. Only the best artists can sketch really well. A sketch differs from what is vulgarly considered finished work, in always acknowledging that there is much beyond what it has recorded, in avowing this quite frankly in the manner of work. To put the matter plainly, any drawing, painting, or etching by Rembrandt, Rubens, or Turner (and many others of the best men), however far it may be carried, always confesses that it might have been carried farther, and though stating some things very plainly, leaves many other things in the stage of mere suggestions. But the artists who do not sketch only give you what they can finish, hinting at nothing that they cannot quite clearly express, saying what they can say clearly, but being silent about what they have not knowledge or leisure to explain. An etcher, therefore, when he works in other arts as a training for his own, ought to avoid these latter methods of work, because etching ought to be not only explanatory of what can be explained, but suggestive of much that cannot be explained.

If I had to train a pupil for etching, especially, I would teach him first to make a good comprehensive pen-drawing, no more imitative of any kind of engraving than my hand-writing as I scribble these pages is imitative of a visiting card, but marking in an honest artistic way the black spaces and the white spaces, and the dots, and shapes, and shades of all kinds, which occur in any fortuitous assemblage of natural objects. In this way he should make sketches, but very careful sketches, that is studies made in a limited time, but hinting at or suggesting much more than could be quite legibly expressed in the time, of men and plants and animals of all kinds, but not of distant landscape, for which this sort of work is of little use. But as the tonality of pen sketches is hardly ever very complete, the pupil should make drawings in sepia, or burnt umber, with a brush for the especial study of tonality, and he should make many of these, giving on the whole about as much time to them as to the pen sketches.

These two things, the pen study for line, and the sepia study for values of light and dark, are sufficient if properly done, and enough done, to educate an etcher. Lalanne makes a great many charcoal drawings; he does them very admirably and very fast, and gets in this way studies both of form and light and shade in the same drawing. It is a very good plan also, but I think on the whole the other, that I have just described, is a better plan for most men, as it separates the two aims of the etcher, linear expression, and tonality.

When you have gone through a great deal of hard study with pen and brush, etch some simple subject, to begin with, from nature, by my positive process, and another subject by the old negative process, and giving each a fair trial. Amuse yourself for a while in trying the different processes described in this book, and if you feel a decided preference for one or the other, have faith in your preference, for it is suggested by your own mental constitution, and practise your own process steadily till you succeed in it, both from nature, and in the etching-room. You will have many a hard battle, many an hour of mortification, but let me tell you that all good etchers have passed through these ordeals, and been dirty with charcoal and oil and printing-ink, and burnt their skin with acid, and spent hours and days in rubbing and scraping and correcting, often with no immediate result except utter disappointment. Correct plates a little, but if they do not come right with a reasonable amount of effort and pains, have them repolished, and etch something else upon them. You will advance better by doing fresh subjects than by wasting time in trying to cure your incurables. Imitate nature in this as in everything. She does not trouble herself about curing incurables, but sends fresh healthy babies every day into the world to replace them; she leaves the uprooted tree to rot where it lies, but all around it the twin-leaved younglings sprout from there cotyledons. Etch many plates innocently and happily, not troubling yourself in the least about what any friends or the public may think about them; then select a few of the best and liveliest of these, to be printed, and send the rest unhesitatingly to the planer.

CHAPTER XVIII.

Vulgar Errors about Etching.

THERE exist many vulgar errors about etching which the student is sure to hear repeated on every side of him from people who are ignorant of the art, and it may be of use to mention a few of them in this place. A writer in the *Morning Post* for August 4, 1868, has kindly done me the service of putting these vulgar errors in print, in an article which consisted of nothing else. For the sake of brevity I will make quotations from the article, and answer them.

1. "'*Of all the arts known to us as yet, etching*,' we are told, '*is the best fitted for the especial purpose of the free expression of artistic thought*,' *but this thought must be purely artistic, not merely intellectual, so that man's noblest distinction, the faculty of thinking, is made inferior and subordinate to the mechanical tact of imitation.*" *

The misunderstanding here is a very common one. The writer sees nothing but imitation in the arts of design, and fancies that by artistic thought we mean nothing but the exercise of the imitative faculty. This is precisely what we do *not* mean. For example, if any painting or etching were simply imitative of nature, no competent critic would allow that there was any artistic thought in it at all. Let me illustrate this by a reference to literature, which, as an art, is much

* The critic in the *Morning Post* is here quoting from 'Etching and Etchers.'

better understood in England than the arts of design are. Any work of literary art, whether the subject of it be derived from invention—as 'Adam Bede'—or from real occurrences, as 'Macaulay's History of England,' is sure to contain a great deal that is above and beyond the simple imitation of nature. If there were nothing beyond the mere selection of materials this would be much already, for the exercise of artistic choice, the mere labour of omission, is a great and high exercise of the human mind. But in books such as the two just mentioned there is much more than the labour of omission; there is the art of presenting things and arranging things so as to produce a certain pre-calculated, pre-determined effect upon the mind of the reader, the art of inducing the reader to see things from the author's point of view, of making him feel the impressions that the author has felt, and prefer what he has preferred. In the novel what there is of imitation of nature is subordinated to artistic invention; in the history we have not so much a narrative of the facts as an artistic presentation of a portion of the facts. In both novel and history there is consummate art in every page, and that is why they are famous. So in the arts of design you have paintings, drawings, etchings, which the ignorant believe to be simply imitative, but which invariably, if they are of any value, have cost much exercise of artistic thought, in choice, omission, arrangement, subtle calculation of result with a view to produce a certain pre-determined impression on the mind of the spectator. All this is quite outside of imitation, and really incompatible with quite strict imitation, yet this is what is meant by fine art, and imitation is not fine art.* Until people clearly understand this, the fine arts are a sealed book to them, because they cannot receive the ideas of men who express themselves by that medium.

Now I have never said that etching was the best art for imitation. I hold it to be on the whole, the best and most convenient of the fine arts for the free expression of artistic ideas, but although very marvellous feats of imitation have been done in it by Boisseau, Charles Jacque, Jules Jacquemart, and one or two others, which prove that wonderful imitative power may be reached in the art, this costs too much labour to be worth the attainment of the painter-etcher, who will find the best use of etching to be the free expression of his thoughts and feelings *about* nature rather than the imitation *of* nature.

2. "*The record is only a collection of lines, by which the artist can delineate only what he has actually seen, and can invent nothing.*"

This assertion that inventions cannot be set down in etching is so contrary to well-known facts in the history of art, besides being inherently so absurd, that it seems hardly worth while to answer it. It may be enough to observe that about one-third of Rembrandt's finest plates *are* pure inventions of scenes which Rembrandt never beheld, such as the 'Crucifixion,' the 'Raising of Lazarus,' and many others, that a considerable number of Turner's etchings, such as his 'Jason' and the 'Dragon,' are pure inventions; that amongst the works of living men the whole of those of Chifflart, and very many etchings by other masters,

---

* Of course imitation might be said to be an art in a lower sense, but it is not fine art.

as Bracquemond for example, are records of thoughts and fancies as far removed from the regions of actual fact as the wildest imaginations of William Blake himself. The assertion that an invention cannot be recorded in etching is inherently absurd, for if it can be recorded in drawing it can be recorded in etching, which *is* drawing.

3. "*There is something beyond etching for which it is but a preparatory move, and the most mechanical of all. All art is essentially mechanical; the needle, the burin, the pencil, the brush—these are all machines or tools worked by the hand to copy what the eye beholds, and the faithfulness of the copy constitutes the merit of the work. No graphic delineation can pourtray the invisible, no artist can figure feeling; this must be extracted by spectators themselves out of the imitated forms, as his was excited by the view of the originals.*"

The writer does not understand the sense in which the words "mechanism" and "mechanical" are commonly employed in art criticism; let me explain it.

Suppose you drew a series of lines with a view to get them perfectly parallel and of perfectly equal thickness, your success in doing this would be a mechanical success, not an artistic one. But supposing, on the other hand, that you drew a number of lines for the purpose of conveying to another mind a notion of some composition which you had just invented in your own, then you would not be working mechanically but artistically, that is, not for a mechanical purpose, but an artistic purpose. So far from being the most mechanical kind of engraving, etching, as we understand it, is the least mechanical, because the true etchers never think about mechanical perfections at all, using lines simply for the expression of artistic thought. Compare for example a sky, etched by any one of the great men, and a sky engraved by the machine-ruler. In the first, the only object is to convey to you an impression of what the artist felt about the sky, without the least pre-occupation about having lines parallel or equidistant, but in the second mechanical perfection is an object in itself. Or compare your own signature, and the same name engraved on your visiting card. There may be a good deal of what goes to constitute genuine etching in an autograph signature, much personal character, and in every gentleman's writing there is an absolute scorn of mechanical perfection. But in the engraved name on a visiting card mechanical perfection is an aim in itself. The hair-strokes must be of the same thickness, for example, and that is a mechanical perfection.

It does not follow that because a man uses a tool he uses it mechanically. The paddles of a steam-ship are tools, and they are used mechanically by the steamengine; the paddle of a canoe is a tool, but it is not used mechanically by a canoist who is descending a difficult rapid. A workman may use tools mechanically or he may not. Whenever his intelligence is continually interfering to modify the action of the tool, he is not working mechanically but intelligently, and if the purpose of his labour is to express ideas of an artistic kind, he is not working mechanically but artistically. We affirm that an etched line, as a good etcher draws it, is less mechanical than a burin line, since its modulations, produced by the operation of the intellect or feeling of the artist, are more numerous and delicate, because the tool is more obedient. On the other hand

VULGAR ERRORS ABOUT ETCHING. 73

the mechanical perfections of the burin line are usually much greater than those of the etched line. The anxiety to attain mechanical perfection would probably injure an etcher by diminishing the spontaneousness of his expression, but it would not injure an engraver, who indeed needs it on account of the nature of his art.

The assertion that in art "the faithfulness of the copy constitutes the merit of the work," is simply an expression of the most prevalent of vulgar errors. Literal copyism is not fine art at all, for it is incompatible with invention, with composition, with selection, and even with the expression of all personal feeling in the artist.

The other assertion that no artist can pourtray the invisible or "figure feeling" displays a deep ignorance of that which is the very essence of all noble art. When an artist paints or etches anything he conveys to all who are in sympathy with him, and that in the very clearest manner possible, the feelings and emotions of his own mind during the hours whilst he was at work, its sadness or its gaiety, its sensitiveness, its preferences, its appreciations. Now the *way* in which he does this is by altering everything he sees, not so much intentionally as inevitably, and the more genius he has, the more he alters everything. In saying this I am not writing a fancy which cannot be proved, but a fact which may be easily demonstrated. Take any first-rate artistic work representing a person or a place, and you will find in it a thousand departures from literal truth, and it is through the kind and degree of these departures that the artist expresses his own sentiment about the theme for which he has composed these variations. I say that literal copyism *is not fine art*, and that the departures from literal truth which are suggested by imagination, by sentiment, by taste, are the true artistic expression, the real essence of art.

It is a mistake to imagine that if the forms of nature were accurately imitated by an artist, you would experience the same emotions in looking at his work that you would have felt, or that he felt, in presence of the natural scene. The contrary has been proved, by actual experiment, over and over again. For example, no photograph or topographical drawing ever conveyed to the spectator the emotion which the spectator had felt, or felt afterwards, in presence of the natural scene. And it is clear that when an artist copies nature literally, excluding the variations which come of emotion, he does not express *his* emotion. The demand for "faithful copying of nature" is a demand for the suppression of the individuality of the artist. Two topographical draughtsmen, perfect in their craft, might produce views of the same scene, both copied faithfully, and therefore both alike; two artists never would.

4. "*Claude is acknowledged to have acquired his renown 'by means of artistic and harmonious composition, and beautiful effects of light,' which are beyond the etcher's reach, and can be compassed only by the painter.*"

The writer here asserts, first, that composition is beyond the reach of the etcher. There are etchings which are not compositions, just as there are pictures which are not compositions, but there are also many etchings which are very complete and beautiful compositions, as much so as the most celebrated pictures. For example, all the etchings of Claude, without

VULGAR ERRORS ABOUT ETCHING. 75

exception, are compositions, and the best of them are as finely composed as the best of all his pictures. All the etchings in Turner's 'Liber Studiorum' are compositions of a very high kind. Most of Rembrandt's religious subjects are compositions, and there is not one of his pictures which displays profounder art in arrangement of material than his etchings of the 'Death of the Virgin' and 'Christ Healing the Sick.' Several living etchers compose very beautifully (especially Charles Jacque), but it is unnecessary to multiply instances. Indeed, it is clear that if an artist can compose in a drawing, he can compose equally well in an etching also.

The other statement, that beautiful effects of light are beyond the etcher's reach, may be answered summarily by a reference to Claude's 'Sunset.' Amongst moderns, Haden has etched beautiful effects of light, Samuel Palmer's effects of early dawn, and sunset, and moonlight, are quite absolutely successful. In France both Appian and Lalanne have given effects of light in etching with great harmony and power. So also has Méryon. So have several etchers of less note.

Other popular errors about etching still remain to be noticed. There exists a very general impression even amongst artists, that etching is "an imperfect art." This impression is due to the great ignorance which prevails with regard to what etchers have actually accomplished, and also to the quantities of poor attempts in etching by painters and others who have never learned it. People who have never heard good violin playing imagine that the violin is an imperfect instrument, tolerable as an accompaniment, not knowing that it is the most perfect solo instrument which exists. So, many people who have not studied good etching believe that it is an imperfect kind of engraving.

Some say it cannot model, others that it cannot imitate the nature of objects, others that it cannot reach true tone. All these things are difficult in etching, but they are not impossible; they are not even more difficult than in other kinds of engraving upon metal. But they are very difficult, impossible even, for men who take up etching as an amusement. Only men who have devoted much time to the art have overcome these difficulties effectually. Rembrandt could model you a face in etching quite as well as professional line-engravers can. Weirotter could get any tone he wanted, just as if he had been drawing in sepia. Jules Jacquemart can express the nature of *substances*, bronze, porphyry, crystal, agate, jasper, lapis lazuli, and express simultaneously the most intricate and difficult forms, from the swelling of a muscle on a tiny silver statuette to the drooping of the petals of a whole bouquet of garden-flowers. All this he does in pure etching, and he does it more exquisitely and more thoroughly than it has ever been done in black and white before, no matter by what species of drawing or engraving. I admit that artists who take up etching as an amusement, not believing it to be capable of much, cannot do anything of this kind, but can they do any better with the burin, in line engraving? No art has ever been so unfairly judged as etching. Artists and others, all of them, so far as etching goes, strictly amateurs, work at etching a week or a fortnight in the year, and then say that the art is imperfect, that

VULGAR ERRORS ABOUT ETCHING. 77

it is incapable of rendering this thing or that. The incapacity lies in the men, and not in the art. What should we say of line-engraving, if it were to be judged of only by the attempts of amateurs? Would the same amateurs who fail with the etching-needle succeed better with the burin, and would it be fair to judge of what the burin can accomplish by the performances of those who have never mastered it?

It will be rather agreeable than otherwise to the persevering student (though not to the indolent one) to be told that when he fails the failure is not due to any imperfection in the art, but to his own want of mastery in it. All that artists care about in black and white art *can be done, has been done*, in etching.

The popular error has been to imagine that etching was an extremely easy, but very imperfect art, and that any one who knew something of drawing had nothing to do but to buy coppers and etch away as fast as he liked. But since the revival of etching which has taken place during the last ten years, the etchers have found out two things, first that the art is vastly more difficult than they fancied it to be, and next that its capabilities are quite beyond anything they dreamed of.*

---

* Painters are so handsomely paid in these days (when they are paid at all) that they naturally neglect etching, which has hitherto not been very productive. However there are hopes of progress in this respect. One of my friends can get fifty pounds for a plate, and another, not long since, realized by one plate six hundred pounds for himself and two hundred for his publisher. When etching becomes as remunerative as water-colour it will be followed by better draughtsmen than the majority of those who at present attempt it, and followed more persistently, and with more uniformly good results.

CHAPTER XIX.

Printing.

EVERY etcher ought to print his own proofs, to learn the state of his plate. It is unnecessary to give a minute account of the printing-press. Small presses of my invention are sold in London by the publisher of this book,* and as for learning to print, the etcher must get some copper-plate printer to teach him. He will learn the art in a dozen lessons.

There are two kinds of printing, artificial and natural. Artificial printing is resorted to, to sustain weak portions of a plate which has not been brought into harmony by the etcher; natural printing consists simply in filling all the lines with printing ink, and cleaning quite perfectly the spaces of smooth copper between them. An etcher who prints need never trouble himself about artificial printing at all, for what he requires is to know the real condition of his plate, not to conceal or counterbalance its deficiencies. You ought never to leave a plate in such an imperfect condition that you cannot get a proper-looking proof without calling to your aid the dodges of artificial printing. Always print quite simply, helping no one portion of your plate more than another; in this way you will learn the plain truth about it, and when you are satisfied with it you will probably also be satisfied

* C. Roberson & Co., 99, Long Acre.

PRINTING. 79

with such copies of it as any honest copper-plate printer will take from it, however little he may know about the fine arts. If, on the other hand, you etch in such a manner that your plate is passable only with highly artificial printing, you will have endless anxieties and vexations, and very likely never find a workman who will treat it quite to your mind. All that can be done by the most cunning artificial printing can be done by the etcher with the etching-needle or the dry point upon the plate itself, and it is much more convenient that he should do it so, more convenient for all parties concerned.

There are several ways of getting (bad) proofs besides printing. You may ink the plate, and then take a cast of it in plaster of Paris; the mould will show the state of the plate more or less accurately. Or you may bathe a sheet of paper in melted white wax, till there is a thin coat of white wax upon it, and then put it on the plate, and rub its back with a burnisher. This will give you a proof if you manage it well, so it is said, at least.* But after all there is nothing like printing, as Rembrandt did, with your own blackened right hand.

I may mention an important improvement in my miniature presses which may easily be added to those already in use. The great objection to those little presses was, that owing to the small circumference of the cylinder it did not rise easily upon the copper, but would sometimes turn round and round upon the cloth without getting upon the copper at all. This incon-

* I never could get a decent proof in this way, not being clever enough.

venience may be entirely obviated by screwing two slips of copper-plate to the travelling board, running the whole length of it, one on each side. The cylinder runs on these, as on rails, and not having to rise much when it meets the plate (only the thickness of the cloths) gets upon it and passes over it with facility. I recommend every reader who has bought one of the miniature presses to have this improvement added.

CHAPTER XX.

Some Notes on Etching Tools.

I HAVE already spoken of the etching-needle elsewhere. It is best to have it heavy, and all in one piece. The etching-needles usually sold are fixed in wooden handles, and become shaky after hard drypoint work. Only have your needle cut to a very acute angle (as a mechanical draughtsman cuts a pencil), or else you will find that the thick iron prevents you often from seeing your lines properly.

When practising the old process it is convenient to have a hand-vice with a wooden handle, as a hand-vice all of metal sometimes becomes inconveniently hot; but this is a mere luxury.

A matter of very great consequence indeed is to learn how to sharpen your dry point properly for drypoint work. It ought to have a short cutting edge, rounded, but cutting, not pointed. When once you have drawn a good dry-point line on the copper, and felt the peculiar feeling in the hand which there is when the tool takes to the copper kindly, examine the point of it with a microscope, and you will see a rounded cutting edge, which (on a very tiny scale) resembles the rounded knife that saddlers use for cutting leather. When once you have seen it (and felt it in working) you will be able afterwards to sharpen it in that way.

G

As for the etching-needles you will sharpen them, or make them blunt, exactly as you require them to be.

The scrapers ought always to be kept *as sharp as possible*. If their edges get broken or blunted they will scratch the copper, and then the task is simply endless. You use the scraper to remove scratches; it makes fresh scratches, you use it again to remove these; it makes fresh ones, and so on *ad infinitum*.

The burnisher is used to *crush* inequalities in the copper, and produce a smooth surface. I use it very little, finding charcoal generally more certain and more convenient. If the reader uses it he must keep it in a state of the highest possible polish, as everything depends upon that. The way to keep a burnisher polished is to have a slip of deal about six inches long, with a groove cut in it with a very small gouge. Then you rub your burnisher to and fro in this little groove, and that keeps it in proper condition.

CHAPTER XXI.

The Illustrations.

IN executing this little series of plates, I have had to contend against a great practical difficulty, for which the intelligent reader will make allowances. It is not possible to change one's process every day and yet do thoroughly good work; hence these little plates, though careful, cannot represent the several processes they illustrate as those processes would be represented by six or seven different artists, devoted specially to each of them. To change from one process to another in the arts of design is almost (though not quite) as bad as changing from one language to another when we speak or write, or from one instrument to another when we perform music; and the task which has been imposed upon me in the illustration of the present volume has been as difficult and wearisome as if I had had to write the pages of it in several different tongues. I mention this, not as an apology for any defects in the plates (for they have not pretension enough to call for apologies), but to warn the student never to judge of any process in etching (or any other branch of the fine arts) by the attempts of men who do not make that particular process their speciality. For however well a man may have known and practised a process formerly, it very soon slips out of his grasp when he has once laid it aside, and he cannot recover it without weeks of patient labour. The great rule for success in etching is to choose a process and stick to it, or, if you leave it for a better, to leave it definitively. Never yield to the delusion that you will be able to practise with efficiency several different kinds of etching in the same month, it cannot even be done in the same year. The mind cannot work freely in any art until the doing of good technical work has become a habit; and, however profound may be your knowledge of nature, you will not be able to acquire good habits in any process which is unfamiliar to you in less than three or four months of practice. In some of the processes of etching there are details which require great patience, in stopping-out for instance, and if you have given up stopping-out (as in my positive process) you will find it very trying to go back to it again; the trouble of it will plague you, and you will do it hastily and imperfectly. Or if you leave the old process for the positive one, you will be frightened at first by having to make calculations about time of biting whilst at work upon the drawing, and this little difficulty will magnify itself into quite a considerable obstacle. Again, there are *manual* difficulties in changing from one process to another, often not to be surmounted without great labour. For example, in passing from etching to dry point, there is a great manual difficulty about feeling the point on the copper which cannot be overcome without much practice.

Plate I. (M) Juniperus Prumos Hills in a feral state.

PLATE I.

Old Negative Process—Plate in a First State.

There were three stoppings-out, and then the plate was cleaned and re-grounded, this time with a transparent ground, in which were drawn the lines of the sky and distance. The difference in value of dark between the large tree-trunk and the more distant trunk to the left is caused by the fact that the paler one was protected by Japan varnish, whilst the other continued exposed to the action of the acid.

But a plate in this state cannot be considered finished. The leafage, for example, is in a good state of preparation for future work, but no more, and the ends of the branches are purposely left fragmentary to leave space for foliage yet to be drawn; it would be desirable, also, to throw a tint over the distance, a pale tint in fine lines very close to each other. The foreground, too, requires some vigorous work to sustain the dark trunk of the beech tree, which greatly wants a basis, as it has a look of being suspended in the air, and this foreground, under the effect of the light, ought to tell as a dark against the sky. Now all these improvements may be added in subsequent states of the plate by using transparent grounds and frequent stoppings-out.

PLATE II.

Old Negative Process, Four Bitings, Retouched with Dry Point.

This plate is carried farther than the preceding one, and there is but little work in it at the stage of mere preparation. We have an instance here of a facility which was convenient in the old negative process, that of stopping-out before the first biting began. The reader will observe a few little twigs in front of the great trunk under the gnarled branch. These twigs have a light side, but this light side was not reserved in shading the trunk, it was stopped-out afterwards before the first biting.

There are differences in tonic value between the branches themselves; this is due to subsequent stoppings-out. The bit of grass at the tree's foot is pure dry point. It would have been possible, of course, to add a tint of sky in pure dry point with the bur removed, behind the branches; but this is merely a study of a tree-trunk.

PLATE III.

Sketch in One Sitting by Hamerton's Positive Process.

In a sketch in one sitting it is not possible to have any very accurate definition of form, on account of the time at your disposal, but you *must* pay attention to the tonic values of the various parts of your com-

Plate 11. Old Negative Forms: four late nips and dry pours

Plate IV. Sketch from Nature in low village by Hammerton. Winter. Pen and washed off-hand. Total Immersion 2½ hours. Thermometer 17.

position. If your time has been properly calculated, the tonality will come right of itself in the positive process. Observe, for instance, in this plate, the difference in value between the iris and alder-bush to the right and the bushes and bank to the left, on the other side of the stream. Again, observe the difference between the bank and the distant trees, and between the nearest of those trees and the hill behind it. All these diferences both in the depth and thickness of the lines were due simply to the time of biting, as the needle employed was the same for all of them, and the hand-pressure precisely equal everywhere.

I may add that I had one of my miniature presses with me at the riverside, and that, within a few minutes after the removal of the plate from the bath, I had taken a proof of it, there, on the grassy bank.

PLATE IV.

Etching in Two Sittings by Hamerton's Positive Process.

In this plate the reader is invited to observe, first, the perfect soundness of the ground, which is not pitted anywhere, notwithstanding its extreme tenuity, and secondly the immense utility of the enlargement of the line. For without that enlargement, the vigorous lines in the foreground would have been as thin as those of the little bush in the extreme distance. Again, you will perceive that the later and thinner lines have been used frequently *as a glaze* over spaces already mapped out by strong indications, such as the roof and eaves of the hut, the arch of the well, the little rustic gate, &c. It is one of the great advantages of the positive process to be able to throw a light tint in this way over a skeleton of firm lines without being obliged to ground the plate over again. In the old negative process, to do this you had to lay a fresh ground, which had to be either black or transparent. If it was black, none but the stronger lines already done remained clearly visible, whereas if it was transparent the lines to be added as a glaze would not be visible to you whilst you were drawing them. In the positive process this kind of glazing is as convenient as the rest of the work, and causes no interruption of any kind.

Although this plate was executed in two sittings, it was not grounded twice. In large elaborate plates the sittings may be renewed as often as you please, on condition of removing the ground and laying a fresh one over the whole plate after every six hours of labour in the bath.

A friend wrote to me the other day and said that he supposed the positive process would be useful only for simple subjects; he had seen a plate by Bracquemond which had been bitten sixty times. Bracquemond, in using the old negative process, stopped-out sixty times, in order to get sixty degrees of depth in his lines. But a plate etched positively in the bath, although no stopping-out is used, passes from dark to pale even more gradually than that, in fact without any steps at all. The continuous bath is equal to sixty bitings, if you will, or to sixty thousand.

Plate 1.

PLATE V.

Two Kids, with Landscape.

I give this plate as an illustration of a particularly safe way of etching, very suitable for beginners. In this instance the order of my positive process was exactly reversed, and the work passed gradually from the palest tones to the darkest, the most intense blacks being reserved for the very last. This plan is a safe one, because if you have any corrections to make during the progress of the work it is always easier to efface a pale line than a dark one, for the pale one is shallow, but the dark one has bitten deeply. I began by sketching the whole subject by the old negative process, and gave it a very light biting, then I grounded the plate afresh with the transparent ground and gave a sitting in the bath of about half an hour. This gave the clouds and distance, and some tints about the foreground. After that I cleaned the plate and grounded it again, giving a longer sitting this time, and so on I proceeded, grounding between the sittings and making the time of immersion longer and longer as I came to the intense darks. Finally I got a little black velvet here and there with the dry point.

This is a dilatory way of proceeding, because the plate requires several days, but it need not occupy much of the artist's time during those days. For example, the last black strokes ought to be immersed six hours, but they may be drawn in a few minutes, and the plate requires no attention whilst it is in the bath. The system of passing from pale to dark is much followed by professional engravers, which shows the prudence of it.

I do not wish to recommend this etching as a model of workmanship. In the sky, it would have been better to rely either upon the outline or the shaded space, but not to give both. Skies are always rather embarrassing in etching, and ought to be frankly treated on one of two principles, either the line, in which case there ought to be no pretension to any but the rudest shading, or else the space, which ought then to be shaded quite delicately, and, if in the old negative process, with great care and labour in stopping-out.

PLATE VI.

A Sketch in Pure Dry Point.

My hand is little accustomed to dry point, which I dislike, not for the effect produced, but for the comparative want of artistic liberty in the instrument. Any etcher of ability, however, who chose to give a year's practice to this kind of engraving, would probably be well rewarded for his labour, since, though not so free as the point in etching, it is more capable of free work than it seems at first, and offers vast resources by the fine quality of its darks, which are fully equal to those of mezzotint. In fact dry point *is* mezzotint in shaded spaces where the bur, more or less reduced by the scraper, gives the dark as it does in mezzotint. The only difference is that the bur in what is called mezzotint is raised by the teeth of the

Plate VI. Three Tiny Pools, the sketches used very sparingly.

berceau, whereas in dry point it is raised by the hatchings of one steel needle. But the dry point is superior to mezzotint in having a line at command, a line the freedom of which lies between that of the burin and that of the etching needle. It draws all fine curves very beautifully, but rebels somewhat against picturesque irregularities. However, the reader may see in the roofs of these cottages that even a broken line may be managed in dry point.

Dry point is an art of which the most has not yet been made. It is not to be supposed that etchers, who draw perhaps two dry-point plates a year, can be said in any complete sense to have mastered its difficulties, whilst, on the other hand, engraver's dry point, not relying upon bur at all, is not the same art. A man of genius who loved dry point, and did nothing else, would get very fine effects indeed.

I may add that a dry point may be done positively or negatively. To do it positively you engrave on the bare copper and very frequently, with a small leather dabber, spread either printing ink or a mixture of tallow and lamp-black upon the plate, wiping it with a bit of printer's canvas. The black remains in the lines, and shows you what you have been doing. It is unpleasant, however, to work upon the bare copper out of doors on account of its glitter, and for dry point work from nature the negative process may be preferred. You simply ground and smoke the plate as if for a negative etching, and then work boldly, not forgetting to raise a sufficient bur. It will usually be found necessary, however, after the first proof is taken, to correct by the positive process which I have just described.

CHAPTER XXII.

Of Finish in Etching.

It may be well to conclude with a few words about finish, which is not very generally understood. In etching it does not consist in the multiplicity of lines. People imagine, when they see few lines, that the work is unfinished, but when they see evidence of great labour, in many strokes of the needle, they praise the work for its high finish. But *the true finish lies in the intensity and successfulness of the mental act*, and that may be proved quite as much by selection and omission as by hand-labour. Always endeavour, in etching, to express your thought in as few lines as may be, and to put as much meaning into each of those few lines as it can possibly be made to convey. The real finish in etching resides there. Finish as the best poets finish their landscape descriptions, where there is not a word too much, and every syllable tells.*

---

* Two opposite kinds of false finish prevail in the contemporary English and French schools of etching. In England, etchers usually finish falsely by the multiplicity of lines which have little meaning; in France, on the other hand, they finish falsely by the meaningless impudence of what ought to be the *capital*, or most expressive lines. We are not in great danger from bad French etching, as its insolence is seen at a glance, and esteemed at its true value. Our danger lies in the other direction, that of laborious, rather than indolent meaninglessness.

ADDENDA.

1. TO ETCH ELABORATE PLATES BY THE POSITIVE PROCESS.

A way in some respects easier and less perplexing than the one suggested already is the following:—

Begin by etching a part of your subject, say the foreground, or a part of the foreground, or one figure. Finish that entirely, going of course from dark lines to light ones and putting each where you want them. When this portion of your subject is quite finished, take the plate out of the acid bath, and dry it carefully between sheets of new and very soft blotting paper. Then apply, with a camel-hair brush, to the part that you have been working upon, a coat of transparent stopping-out varnish. This will protect what you have been doing against the further action of the acid, and still allow you to see it with reference to future work. In this way you may gradually go over a very elaborate plate.

2. TO ETCH A PLATE BY THE POSITIVE PROCESS, BEGINNING WITH THE PALE LINES AND GOING GRADUALLY TO DARKER ONES.

Sketch the whole subject lightly, finishing only those parts which are to be palest. Then remove the plate from the bath, and dry it with blotting-paper. Apply another coat of wax solution. This will fill all the lines and protect them from further biting. When the wax is dry, immerse again in the bath, and proceed with lines that are to be somewhat darker. Apply another coat of wax solution, and so on till you get down to the darkest lines, which are done last.

This way of proceeding is slow (see description of Plate V.) and unsuitable for working from nature, but for plates done at leisure in the house it has certain advantages, especially when the etcher is not quite sure of himself.

3. SPECKS AND ROTTEN LINES.

In the old negative process specks and rotten lines occur rather frequently, even in plates by the greatest masters. The great masters were rather tolerant of them, looking to expression always, and forgiving themselves these technical blemishes. Specks occur when the ground is porous, and rotten lines when the ground has not been entirely and clearly removed by the needle in its passage upon the copper. To avoid them, pay great attention to the chemical quality of your ground, to its degree of hardness, and to the regularity of your hand pressure when at work. The way you smoke the ground, in the old negative process, may have a good deal to do with it. It is one of the many advantages of my positive process that neither specks nor rotten lines occur in it, the perfection of the wax ground, applied equally in solution and not afterwards endangered by smoking, ensures you against specks, whilst rotten lines are effectually prevented by the sharpness of the needle which is used for thick and thin lines alike.

THE END.

DRYDEN PRESS:
J. DAVY AND SONS, 137, LONG ACRE, LONDON.

CATALOGUE

OF

MATERIALS FOR DRAWING,

PAINTING, &c.

CHARLES ROBERSON,

Artists' Colour Maker,

No. 99, LONG ACRE,

LONDON.

DRYDEN PRESS:
J. DAVY AND SONS, LONG ACRE, LONDON.

INDEX.

	PAGE.		PAGE.
Academy Boards	25	Crayons, French	11
Aluminium Shells	6	Crow Quills and Pens	32
Artists' Pocket Knives	29	Curves and Angles	18
" Studio Easels	19	Dippers for Oil	29
Badger Hair Softeners	28	Drawing Boards, Deal	18
Blocks of Drawing Paper	8	" Mahogany	18
" Prepared Paper for Oil	25	Drawing Papers, Whatman's	7
Boxwood for Engraving	32	" Harding's	7
Boxes of Oil Colours	23 and 24	" Cartridge	7
" Cake Colours	2	" Imitation Creswick	7
" Moist & Tube Colours	3 and 4	" Tinted Crayon	7
Brown Sable Pencils	12	Drawing Pencils	11
" " in ferrules for Water Colour	13	" Pins	11
Brush Washers	29	" and Sketch Books	9
Brushes for Water Colour Painting	12 to 15	Easels	19 and 20
Brushes for Oil Painting	26 to 27	Engraving Tools	31
Cabinet Saucers	16	Etching Materials	31
Cake Colours	1	Flat Camel Hair Brushes, for Washes	15
Camel Hair Pencils	15	Folding Easels	20
" Brushes in Tin for Water Colour	14 and 15	" Palettes	30
Canvas for Oil Painting, prepared in Rolls	25	French Camel Hair Pencils	15
Canvas on Frames	25	" Tracing Paper	7
Cartoon Paper	7	Gilders' Knives	30
Cartridge Paper	7	" Tips	30
Chalk Pencils	11	" Materials	30
Chalks for Drawing	11	Glass Medium	5
Charcoal	31	Gold Paint	6
China Palettes	17	" Papers	6
" Ink Slabs	17	" Powder	6
" Division Tiles	17	" Shells and Saucers	6
" Saucers	17	" Size	6
Chinese White, in Bottles	5	Gum Water	5
Continuous Paper	7	Hog Hair Brushes, flat	26
Crayon Holders	11	" Varnish Brushes	28
" Paper	7	Illuminating Colours and Materials	6
		Indian Ink	16
		" Rubber	11

INDEX.

	Page
Ivory Palette Knives	29
Japanned Moist Colour Boxes	4
,, Fitted with Colours	3
,, Oil Colour Boxes	23 & 24
,, Plated and Tin Water Bottles and Cups	6
,, Tin Dippers for Oil	29
Lay Figures	30
,, Wooden	30
Lead Pencils	11
Leather Pencil Cases	11
Liquid Indian Ink	5
,, Colours	5
,, Gold Ink	6
,, Cement	5
Lithographic Chalks	32
,, Ink	32
London Boards	10
Mahogany Prepared Panels	25
,, Drawing Boards	18
,, Sketching Boards	18
Mathematical Instruments	18
,, Curves	18
Medium, Roberson's, for Oil Painting	22
Medium, Paris's	22
Millboards, prepared for Oil Painting	25
Moist Water Colours, in Pans	1
,, in Tubes	1
Mounting Boards	10
Oil Sketching Paper	25
,, ,, Books	25
,, Colour Brushes	27
,, Colours in Tubes	21
,, Colour Boxes	23 and 24
Oils, Varnishes, &c.	22
Ox Gall, prepared in Pots	5
Ox Gall, liquid in Bottles	5
Palette Knives	29
Palettes, China	16
,, Mahogany	30
Panels for Oil Painting	25
Parallel Rules	18
Pencils, Chalk	11
,, Lead	11
Pencil Cases	11
Pens for Etching	32
Picture Lining	30
Polished Lead Pencils	11
Portable Seats	20
,, Easels	20
Porte Crayons	11
Portfolios	10
Prepared Canvas	25
,, Millboards	25
,, Panels	25
,, Paper	25
Rack Easels	20
Roberson's Medium	22
,, Liquid Indian Ink	5
Sable Brushes for Water Colour	12 to 14
,, for Oil	27
Sketch Books	9
Sketching Seats and Easels	20
,, Tents	20
,, Umbrellas	20
Solid Sketch Books	9
Studio Easels	19
Stumps	11
Table Easels	20
Tin Dippers for Oil	29
,, Brush Pans	29
,, ,, Washers	29
Tracing Cloth and Paper	7
Transfer Papers, "Black and Coloured"	7
Turnbull's Boards	10
Varnishes	22
Varnish Brushes	28
Water Bottles	6
,, Colour Brushes	12 to 15
Whatman's Drawing Papers	7
Winding Easels	19

CHARLES ROBERSON & CO.'S
WATER COLOURS,
PREPARED IN CAKES, MOIST IN PANS, AND IN TUBES.

Genuine Ultramarine... ...	21s. each.	
Ultramarine Ash	⎫	
Burnt Carmine	⎪	
Gallstone	⎬ 5s. each.	
Madder Carmine...	⎪	
Purple Madder	⎪	
Smalt	⎭	
Aureolin	⎫	
Cadmium	⎪	
Carmine	⎪	
French Ultramarine	⎪	
Green Oxide of Chromium..	⎪	
Emerald ditto ditto ...	⎪	
Extract Vermilion	⎪	
Intense Blue	⎬ 3s. each.	
Lemon Yellow	⎪	
Malachite Green...	⎪	
Mars Yellow	⎪	
Orange Vermilion	⎪	
Pink Madder	⎪	
Rose Madder	⎪	
Yellow Madder	⎪	
Scarlet	⎭	
Cobalt Blue	⎫ 2s. each.	
Violet Carmine	⎭	
Brown Madder	⎫	
Cerulium Blue	⎪	
Crimson Lake	⎪	
Indian Yellow	⎪	
Purple Lake	⎬ 1s. 6d. ea.	
Roman Sepia	⎪	
Scarlet Vermilion	⎪	
Scarlet Lake	⎪	
Sepia	⎪	
Warm Sepia	⎭	

Antwerp Blue	⎫
Bistre	⎪
Brown Oker...	⎪
Brown Pink...	⎪
Burnt Siena...	⎪
Burnt Umber	⎪
Chinese White	⎪
Chrome Yellow	⎪
Constant White	⎪
Deep Chrome	⎪
Dragon's Blood	⎪
Emerald Green	⎪
Flake White	⎪
Gamboge	⎪
Hooker's Green, No. 1 & 2..	⎪
Indigo	⎪
Indian Red	⎪
Ivory Black...	⎪
Lamp Black...	⎬ 1s. each
Light Red	⎪
Naples Yellow	⎪
Neutral Tint	⎪
Olive Green...	⎪
Orange Chrome	⎪
Payne's Grey	⎪
Prussian Blue	⎪
Prussian Green	⎪
Raw Siena	⎪
Raw Umber...	⎪
Roman Oker	⎪
Sap Green	⎪
Terre Verte	⎪
Vandyke Brown	⎪
Venetian Red	⎪
Vermilion	⎪
Yellow Oker	⎪
Yellow Lake	⎭

MOIST WATER COLOURS
IN CHINA PANS AND COLLAPSIBLE TUBES.

THE ABOVE ALSO IN HALF CAKES AND HALF PANS AT HALF PRICE.

WATER COLOUR CAKES IN BOXES.

	£.	s.	d.
Mahogany slide top Box, French polished, Six Colours and Brushes	0	7	0
Ditto Twelve ditto	0	12	0
Small Mahogany Box, with Lock, Twelve Cakes, Brushes and Pencils	0	15	0
Ditto ditto, with Drawer and Saucers	0	17	0
Ditto ditto, Eighteen Colours, ditto	1	1	0
Mahogany Box, Lock and Drawer, Twelve Colours, Ink Slab, Water Glass, Brushes, Pencils, &c.	1	1	0
Ditto ditto, Eighteen Colours, ditto	1	11	6
Ditto ditto, Twenty-four ditto	2	2	0

CADDY LID BOXES.

	£	s.	d.
Small Mahogany Box, Twelve Colours, Ink Slab, Water Glass, Palette, Brushes, Pencils, &c.	1	12	0
Large ditto, Eighteen Colours, ditto	2	12	6
Ditto ditto, with Chalks, &c., complete	3	3	0
Ditto ditto, Twenty-four Colours, ditto	3	13	6
Small Rose-wood Box, Twelve Colours, Palette, Brushes, Pencils, &c., brass bound	2	12	6
Large ditto, Twelve Colours, ditto, Tin Box, with Chalks, Stumps, Porte Crayon, &c., ditto	3	3	0
Ditto ditto, Eighteen Colours, including Carmine, & Smalt	4	14	6
Ditto ditto, Twenty-four Colours, ditto, &c., very complete for hot climates	5	5	0

Also to be had in Half Cakes.

JAPANNED TIN SKETCHING BOXES, FILLED WITH MOIST COLOURS.

Selections of Colours in general use by Water Colour Artists.

3	Cake Box.	—For Light and Shade Drawings on Tinted Paper.	Price	8s. 6d.
6	,,	—Assorted for Landscape Painting.	,,	10s. 6d.
6	,,	—Landscape and Figures.	,,	12s. 0d
8	,,	—Landscape.	,,	14s. 0d.
8	,,	—Landscape and Figures.	,,	16s. 0d.
10	,,	—Landscape.	,,	16s. 6d.
10	,,	—Landscape and Figures.	,,	18s. 6d.
12	,,	—Landscape.	,,	19s. 6d.
12	,,	—Landscape and Figures.	,,	22s. 6d.
14	,,	—Landscape.	,,	22s. 6d.
14	,,	—Landscape and Figures.	,,	25s. 6d.
16	,,	— ,, ,,	,,	29s. 0d.
18	,,	—Landscape, Figures and Flowers.	,,	33s. 6d.
20	,,	— ,, ,, ,,	,,	45s. 0d.
24	,,	—Complete for Landscape, Flowers & Figures.	,,	53s. 6d.

12 Half Cake Boxes . . . . 12s each.

QUARTER CAKE BOXES.

6 Quarter Cake Boxes	.	.	.	5s.	,,
8 ,, ,,	.	.	.	6s.	,,
12 ,, ,,	.	.	.	7s. 6d.	,,
18 ,, ,,	.	.	.	12s.	,,

JAPANNED TIN BOXES, FITTED WITH MOIST WATER COLOURS, in Collapsible Tubes.

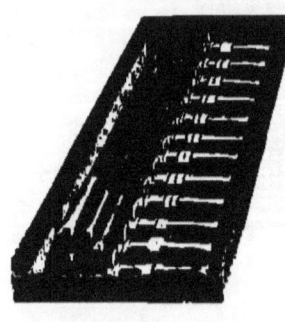 

		£	s.	d.
Japanned Box, folding indented Palette Lid, and Divisions, with 12 Tube Colours		1	1	0
ditto 14 ditto		1	4	0
ditto 16 ditto		1	8	0
ditto 18 ditto		1	15	0
ditto 24 ditto		2	5	0

EMPTY JAPANNED BOXES for MOIST COLOURS, in Pans.

	s.	d.		s.	d.
To hold 4 Cakes	3	6	To hold 14 Cakes	6	0
,, 6 ,,	4	0	,, 16 ,,	6	6
,, 8 ,,	4	6	,, 18 ,,	7	0
,, 10 ,,	5	0	,, 20 ,,	7	6
,, 12 ,,	5	6	,, 24 ,,	9	0

EMPTY JAPANNED BOXES for MOIST COLOURS, in Tubes,

To contain 12 Tubes, with folding Palette plain, 5s. 6d.; 14—6s. 6d.; 16—7s.; 18—7s. 6d.

To contain 12 Tubes, with Divisions and Hollow Flap, 6s. 6d.; 14—7s.; 16—7s. 6d.; 18—8s. 6d.

ROBERSON'S LIQUID INK.

		s.	d.
For Architectural Drawing	per Bottle	1	6

CHINESE WHITE,
IN BOTTLES,
1s.

	s.	d.
Indelible Brown Ink	1	6
Liquid Brown	1	0
Ordinary Colours	1	0
Crimson Lake and Indian Yellow	1	6
Carmine	2	0

PREPARED OX GALL.

In covered Pots . . . . 6d. and 1 0

COLOURLESS LIQUID GALL.

In Bottles 1 0

LIQUID CEMENT AND GUM WATER.

For Mounting Drawings, Prints, &c. . per Bottle 6d. and 1 0

WATER COLOUR and GLASS MEDIUM, used in Coloring Photographs and for giving Brilliancy to Colors.

BOXES AND MATERIALS

FOR

Illumination and Missal Painting.

Colours, Gold and Aluminium Shells, Gold Paper, Agate Burnisher, Sable Brushes, &c., in Boxes, from One Guinea to Five Guineas each.

GOLD AND SILVER SHELLS, SAUCERS, &c.

		s.	d.
Gold in Shells and Saucers	from 6d. to	5	0
In Cakes	„	6	0
Silver in Shells		0	6
Aluminium, ditto		0	6
In Cakes		2	0
Liquid Gold, and Silver in Bottles		1	0
Pure Gold Powder	per Packet	5	0
Silver ditto	„	2	0
Gold Paper	per Sheet	3	6
Bessemer's Gold Paint and Liquid	in Bottles	1	6

JAPANNED BOTTLES AND CUPS FOR WATER.

No. 1—2s. 6d.   No. 2—3s. 0d.   No. 3—3s. 6d. each.
Ditto, plated inside, 4s. 6d., 5s. 6d., and 6s. 6d.

WHATMAN'S DRAWING PAPERS,

Plain or Rolled Surface.

	in.	in.		s.	d.
Demy	20 by	15	*per Sheet*	0	2
Medium	22 „	17	„	0	3
Royal	24 „	19	„	0	4
Imperial	30 „	22	„	0	6
„ Thick	„	„	„	0	9
„ Extra Thick	„	„	„	1	0
„ „ Seamless	„	„	:1	1	3
Double Elephant	40 by	27	„	1	0
Ditto, Extra Thick	„	„	„	2	0
Antiquarian	53 by	31	„	4	0

IMITATION CRESWICK PAPER.

Imperial Size, Extra Thick	30 by	22	*per Sheet*	1	0
Double Elephant, ditto	40 „	27	„	2	0

J. D. HARDING'S PURE DRAWING PAPER.

Imperial	30 by	22	*per Sheet*	0	6
Ditto, Extra Thick	„	„	„	1	0

DRAWING CARTRIDGE.

Imperial	30 by	22	*per Sheet*	0	3
„ Stout	30 „	22	„	0	4

TINTED CRAYON DRAWING.

Imperial Machine-made	30 by	22	*per Sheet*	0	4
Imperial Hand-made	30 „	22	„	0	6

CARTOON PAPERS, 3 ft. 9, 4 ft. 6, & 5 ft. wide . . *from* 1s *per yard.*
„ „ TINTED.

TRACING & TRANSFER PAPERS, & TRACING CLOTH.

TRACING PAPER, 30 by 20, 40 by 30, and 60 by 40 6d., 1s. & 2s. *per Sheet.*
  DITTO in roll 22 yards long, 44 inches wide, *of different thickness.*
TRACING CLOTH, *with dull surface to take ink,* 18, 30, 36, 41 inches wide . . . . . . *from* 1s. *per yard.*

ROBERSON & Co.'s SOLID SKETCH BOOKS,
WHATMAN'S OR HARDING'S EXTRA THICK PAPERS.

					Blocks only. £. s. d.	Cases with Pocket. £. s. d.
Imperial	16mo.	Size	7 by 5 in. in.	. each	0 2 4	... 0 3 9
Ditto	8vo.	„	10 „ 7	. „	0 4 6	... 0 6 3
Ditto	4to.	„	14 „ 10	. „	0 9 0	... 0 12 0
Ditto	half	„	20 „ 14	. „	0 18 0	... 1 4 0
Dble. Elephant	16mo.	„	9 „ 6	. „	0 4 6	... 0 6 0
Ditto	8vo.	„	12 „ 9	. „	0 9 0	... 0 12 0
Ditto	4to.	„	18 „ 12	. „	0 18 0	... 1 4 0

SOLID SKETCH BOOKS OF WHITE OR TINTED PAPERS.

Imperial	16mo.	Size	7 by 5	. each	0 1 10	... 0 3 3
Ditto	8vo.	„	10 „ 7	. „	0 3 3	... 0 5 0
Ditto	4to.	„	14 „ 10	. „	0 6 6	... 0 9 6
Ditto	half	„	20 „ 14	. „	0 12 6	... 0 18 6

These Books are made of selected paper, compressed so as to form an apparently solid substance; the leaves are to be separated by passing a knife round the edges of the uppermost sheet of paper.

SOLID HALF BOUND SKETCH BOOKS.

		in.	in.		s.	d.
Imperial	32mo.	Size 5 by 3¼		each	2	0
Ditto	20mo.	,, 7 ,, 4		,,	2	6
Ditto	16mo.	,, 7 ,, 5		,,	2	9
Ditto	12mo.	,, 8¾ ,, 5¼		,,	3	6
Ditto	10mo.	,, 9½ ,, 6		,,	4	0
Ditto	8vo.	,, 10 ,, 7		,,	4	9
Ditto	4to.	,, 14 ,, 10		,,	8	6

Extra Thick Paper.

Imperial	8vo.	,, 10 ,, 7	. . . .	,,	6	6
Ditto	4to.	,, 14 ,, 10	. . . .	,,	10	6

These Books are bound round the edges similar to the blocks, but only on three sides, the fourth being sewn, so that when cut round the edges, they form a half bound book.

DRAWING AND SKETCH BOOKS,
White and Tinted Papers.

							Half-bound, 32 Leaves.			Stitched, 23 Leaves.		
			in.		in.		£	s.	d.	£	s.	d.
Demy	8vo.	Size	7	by	4¼	. . . each	0	2	0	0	0	8
Ditto	4to.	,,	9	,,	7	. . . ,,	0	3	6	0	1	3
Medium	8vo.	,,	8¼	,,	5¼	. . . ,,	0	2	6	0	1	0
Ditto	4to.	,,	10	,,	8	. . . ,,	0	4	0	0	1	6
Royal	8vo.	,,	9	,,	5½	. . . ,,	0	3	3	0	1	3
Ditto	4to.	,,	11	,,	9	. . . ,,	0	5	0	0	2	6
Imperial	32mo.	,,	5	,,	3¼	. . . ,,	0	1	6			
Ditto	20mo.	,,	7	,,	4	. . . ,,	0	2	0			
Ditto	16mo.	,,	7¼	,,	5½	. . . ,,	0	2	4			
Ditto	12mo.	,,	8¾	,,	5¼	. . . ,,	0	3	0			
Ditto	10mo.	,,	9½	,,	6	. . . ,,	0	3	3			
Ditto	8vo.	,,	10	,,	7	. . . ,,	0	4	3	0	1	9
Ditto	4to.	,,	14½	,,	10	. . . ,,	0	7	0	0	3	6
Ditto	4to.	,,	14½	,,	10,	16 *Leaves* . ,,	.	.	.	0	2	6

PORTFOLIOS,

With Leather Backs and Corners.

	in. in.		Paper Sides.		Cloth Sides.	
			Plain.	With Flaps.	Plain.	With Flaps.
			s. d.	s. d.	s. d.	s. d.
Imperial 4to	15 by 11	each	2 4	3 4	2 6	3 6
Half Royal	19 „ 12½	„	3 4	4 8	4 0	5 3
„ Imperial	22 „ 16	„	5 0	6 6	5 6	7 0
Demy	21 „ 15½	„	4 4	5 8	4 10	6 2
Medium	22 „ 17	„	5 4	6 10	5 8	7 2
Royal	25 „ 19	„	6 6	8 6	7 6	9 6
Imperial	31 „ 22	„	10 6	13 6	13 0	16 0
Atlas	34 „ 26	„	15 0	19 0	16 0	20 0
Double Elephant	40 „ 28	„	24 0	30 0	26 0	32 0

Larger Portfolios and Guard Books made to order.

Improved Portfolio Stands for shewing Drawings.

TURNBULL'S SUPERFINE LONDON DRAWING BOARDS.

	in. in.		2 Sheet.	3 Sheet.	4 Sheet.	6 Sheet.
			s. d.	s. d.	s. d.	s. d.
Foolscap	Size 15 by 12	each	0 5	0 6	0 8	1 0
Demy	„ 18 „ 14	„	0 7	0 10	1 2	1 8
Medium	„ 20½ „ 15½	„	0 9	1 2	1 6	2 3
Royal	„ 22 „ 17½	„	1 0	1 6	2 0	3 0
Imperial	„ 28 „ 20	„	2 0	3 0	4 0	6 0

TURNBULL'S WHITE AND COLOURED MOUNTING BOARDS.

	in. in.		3 Sheet.	4 Sheet.	6 Sheet.	9 Sheet.
			s. d.	s. d.	s. d.	s. d.
Demy	Size 18 by 14	each	0 5	0 6	0 8	1 0
Royal	„ 22 „ 17½	„	0 7	0 9	1 0	1 4
Imperial	„ 28 „ 20	„	1 0	1 3	1 9	2 3
Atlas	„ 31½ „ 24½	„	2 6	3 0	4 6	5 6
Double Elephant	„ 38 „ 25	„	3 0	4 0	5 6	7 0

CUT OUT MOUNTS AND PASSE PARTOUTS.

ROBERSON & CO.'S CUMBERLAND LEAD PENCILS.

		s.	d.
Marked H, HH, HHH, HB, F, B, BB, FF	each	0	6
BBB Very black broad Lead	"	1	0
EHB Ditto HB, ditto ditto	"	1	0
HHHH Extremely hard, for drawing on Wood	"	1	0
BBBB Very black, with extra thick Lead	"	2	0

ROBERSON'S POLISHED CEDAR PENCILS.

		s.	d.
HHH, HH, H, F, HB, B, BB, BBB, EHB	each	0	3
HHHH, HHHHHH, and BBBB	"	0	6

LEATHER PENCIL CASES.

		s.	d.
Round	1s. 1s. 3d., &	1	6
Flat	1s. 6d., 2s. 6d., &	3	0
Roll-up Cases for Pencils, Brushes, &c.		2	6
Ditto, large size		3	6

BLACK, WHITE AND RED CHALKS FOR DRAWING.
CONTÉ CRAYONS & PENCILS.   CHALK PENCILS.
FRENCH COLOURED CRAYONS.

		s.	d.
Boxes containing 1 dozen		1	6
Ditto 1½ "		2	3
Ditto 2 "		3	0
Ditto 3 "		4	6

SOFT FRENCH CRAYONS.

	£.	s.	d.			£.	s.	d.
Box containing 28	0	4	0	Box containing 64		0	14	0
Ditto 46	0	6	6	Ditto 128		1	0	0
Ditto 56	0	10	0	Ditto 164		1	16	0

PORTE CRAYONS, STUMPS, &c.

BRASS PINS FOR FASTENING DOWN PAPER.
INDIAN RUBBER & INK ERASERS.

WATER COLOUR SABLE HAIR BRUSHES,
Of Finest Quality, Tied with Gold Wire.

6d. each.

8d. each.

1s. each.

2s. each.

3s. each.

4s. each.

6s. each.

8s. each.

10s. each.

15s. each.

ROUND AND FLAT SABLES FOR WATER COLOUR.

FLAT.   ROUND.

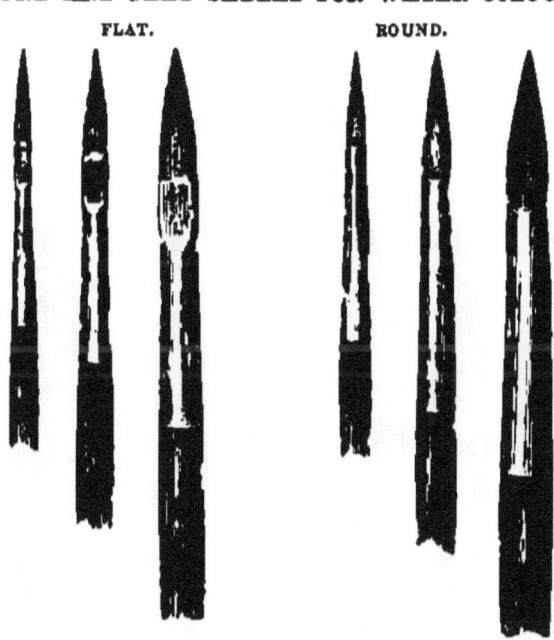

FINEST RED SABLES IN TIN.
FLAT OR ROUND.

	s. d.		s. d.
No. 1	1 0	No. 7	3 0
,, 2	1 2	,, 8	3 9
,, 3	1 4	,, 9	4 6
,, 4	1 6	,, 10	6 0
,, 5	1 10	,, 11	7 6
,, 6	2 3	,, 12	9 0

FINEST BROWN SABLES IN TIN.
ROUND.

	s. d.		s. d.
No. 1	0 8	No. 6	2 3
,, 2	0 9	,, 7	3 0
,, 3	1 0	,, 8	4 6
,, 4	1 3	,, 9	6 0
,, 5	1 6	,, 10	7 6

FINEST BROWN SABLES IN TIN.

FLAT.

		s. d.			s. d.
No. 1 .	. . each	0 8	No. 7 . .	. each	2 6
,, 2 .	. . ,,	0 9	,, 8 . .	. ,,	3 0
,, 3 .	. . ,,	1 0	,, 9 . .	. ,,	4 0
,, 4 .	. . ,,	1 3	,, 10 . .	. ,,	5 0
,, 5 .	. . ,,	1 6	,, 11 . .	. ,,	6 0
,, 6 .	. . ,,	2 3	,, 12 . .	. ,,	7 6

FINEST CAMEL HAIR BRUSHES.

Same Pattern as the Sable Brushes above.

	s. d.		s. d.		s. d.
No. 6 .	0 10	No. 8 . .	1 2	No. 10 . .	1 9
,, 7 .	1 0	,, 9 . .	1 4	,, 12 . .	2 0

FLAT CAMEL HAIR BRUSHES,

For Skies, Washes, &c.

1s. 6d. each.

FLAT CAMEL HAIR BRUSHES.

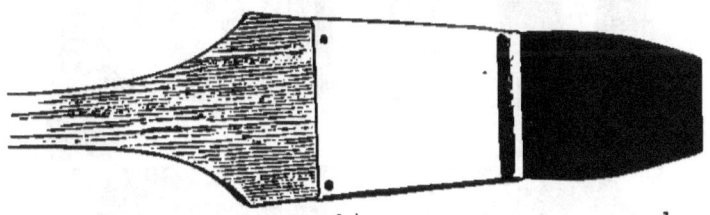

		s.	d.			s.	d.
½ Inch wide	each	0	6	1½ Inch wide	each	1	2
¾ ditto	,,	0	8	1¾ ditto	,,	1	4
1 ditto	,,	0	9	2 ditto	,,	1	6
1¼ ditto	,,	1	0	3 ditto	,,	2	3

FINEST CAMEL HAIR PENCILS,

French Pattern, Tied with Blue and Silver Wire.

		s.	d.
Best Quality, sorted	per dozen	3	0
Crow Quill	each	0	2
Duck Quill	,,	0	3
Goose Quill	,,	0	4
Large Goose Quill	,,	0	6
Extra Small Swan Quill	,,	0	9
Swan Quill, Small	,,	1	3
Ditto, Middle	,,	1	6
Ditto, Large	,,	2	6

INDIAN INK.

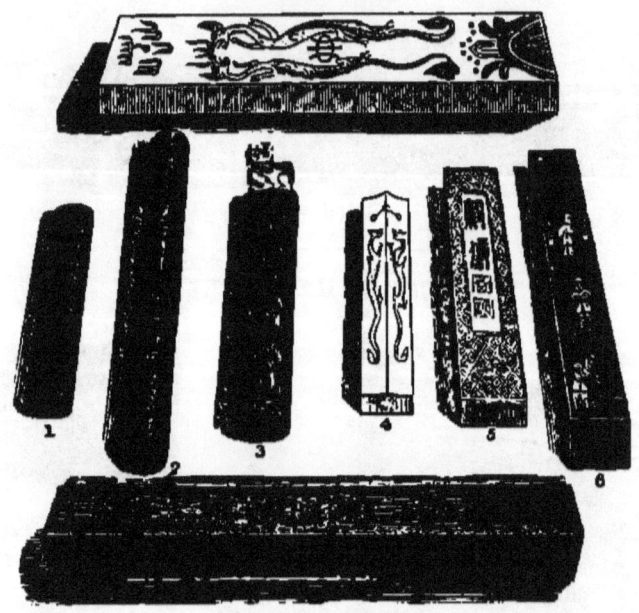

9d. to 7s. 6d. per Stick.

INDIAN INK AND COLOUR SLABS.

1s. and  1s. 6d. each.

CABINET SAUCERS,  Six in the Set.

	s.	d.
No. 1 Set . . . . each	1	8
,, 2 ,, ... ,,	2	3
,, 3 ,, ... ,,	2	9
Leather Cases for ditto . . . each 1s. 6d., 2s. 0d., &	2	6
Tinting Saucers . . . . . per dozen, 1s. to	3	0
Plain China Tiles, 4, 5, 6, 7, 8 & 9 in. Square . . per inch	0	2

FLAT DIVISION CHINA TILES.

6d. to  2s. 6d. each.

SLANT CHINA TILES.

8d. to 3s. 6d. 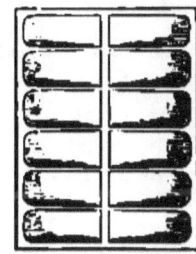  each.

CHINA PALETTES, &c.

3 in. to 10 in. 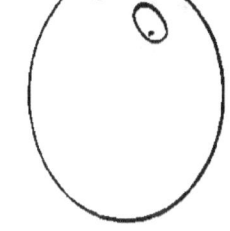 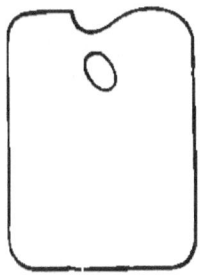 6d. to 1s. 9d. each.

CHINA WELL SLABS.

		s.	d.
3 Wells	each	1	9
5 ,,	,,	2	0
7 ,, as above	,,	2	6

IMPROVED MAHOGANY SKETCHING BOARDS,
With Hinged Frame and Pins.

	in.	in.		£.	s.	d.
Imperial 8vo.	11 by	7½	each	0	7	6
Ditto 4to	15 „	10½	„	0	12	6
Half Imperial	21½ „	15	„	0	14	0

DEAL DRAWING BOARDS.

	in.	in.		£.	s.	d.
4to. Royal	12 by	9½	each	0	1	9
4to. Imperial	16 by	12	„	0	2	6
Half Royal	19 „	12	„	0	2	9
Demy	20 „	15	„	0	3	6
Half Imperial	22 „	16	„	0	4	0
Medium	22 „	17	„	0	4	0
Royal	24 „	19	„	0	5	0
Imperial	31 „	22	„	0	7	6

MAHOGANY DRAWING BOARDS,
With Moveable Panels.

	in.	in.		£.	s.	d.
Demy 4to.	8 by	6	each	0	4	6
Royal 4to.	10½ „	8	„	0	5	6
Imperial 4to.	13½ „	9½	„	0	6	0
Half Medium	15 „	11	„	0	8	0
Demy	18 „	13½	„	0	10	0
Half Imperial	19½ „	13½	„	0	10	6
Royal	22 „	17½	„	0	14	0
Imperial	28 „	19	„	1	1	0

MATHEMATICAL CURVES & ANGLES, 10d. to 3s. each.

EBONY PARALLEL RULES.

Cases **MATHEMATICAL INSTRUMENTS**, from 4s. to £6 6s.

ARTISTS' STUDIO EASELS,
With Single and Double Fronts, Screw Action, &c.

From £3. 10s. to £15. 15s.

DEAL AND MAHOGANY EASELS.

		£	s.	d.
Deal Sketching Easels	each	0	6	0
Deal Standing Easels	,,	0	14	0
Deal Closing Easels	,,	0	8	0
Ditto, to fold	,,	0	16	0
Ditto (with Pegs and Rest Stick enclosed)	,,	1	1	0
,, dwarf Back	,,	1	10	0
Mahogany Closing Easels	,,	0	14	0
,, to fold	,,	1	2	0
,, Standing Easels	,,	0	18	0
,, Rack ditto	,,	3	3	0
Deal Table Easels, with pegs	,,	0	6	0
Mahogany ditto	,,	0	8	0
Deal Rack	,,	0	10	6
Mahogany	,,	0	16	0
Folding Sketching Easels	,,	0	5	0
Walnut, with sliding legs for uneven ground	,,	0	18	0

IMPROVED MAHOGANY RACK EASEL,

With addition of **Shifting Desk, for Oil or Water Color Painting,**

PORTABLE SEATS, &c. FOR SKETCHING

From 5s. to 18s. each.

		£	s.	d.
Sketching Seat and Easel, combined		1	1	0
Ditto, with Shifting Easel, for Sketching, in either Oil or Water		1	10	0
Sketching Umbrellas	each	1	5	0
,, Larger	,,	1	13	0
,, Extra strong	,,	2	6	0
,, With Tent complete	,,	4	0	0
Sketching Tent	,,	2	10	0
Ditto, square	,,	3	0	0

OIL COLOUR MATERIALS.

OIL COLOURS IN COLLAPSIBLE TUBES.

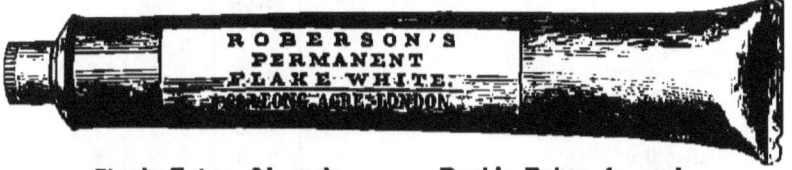

Single Tubes, 6d. each.

- Antwerp Blue
- Asphaltum
- Bitumen
- Black Lead
- Blue Black
- Bone Brown
- Brown Pink
- Brown Red
- Brown Oker
- Burnt Siena
- Burnt Umber
- Caledonian Brown
- Cappah Brown
- Chrome Yellow
- Cologne Earth
- Crimson Lake
- Deep Chrome
- Emerald Green
- Flake White
- Gamboge
- Golden Oker
- Indigo
- Indian Red
- Indian Lake
- Italian Pink
- Ivory Black
- Lamp Black
- Lake
- Light Red
- Mineral Grey
- Mummy
- Naples Yellow
- Naples Yellow, deep
- Olive Lake

Double Tubes, 1s. each.

- Orange Chrome
- Patent Yellow
- Permanent Blue
- Prussian Blue
- Purple Lake
- Raw Siena
- Raw Umber
- Roman Oker
- Scarlet Lake
- Sugar Lead
- Terre Verte
- Vandyke Brown
- Venetian Red
- Verdigris
- Verona Brown
- Yellow Lake
- Yellow Oker

EXTRA COLOURS.

	£	s	d
Ultramarine . . each	1	1	0
Ultramarine Ashes . ,,	0	3	0
Madder Carmine . ,,	0	5	0
Cadmium, pale & deep ,,	0	3	0
Aureolin . . . . ,,	0	3	0
Carmine . . . . ,,	0	3	0
Crimson Madder . ,,	0	3	0
Purple Madder . . ,,	0	3	0
Scarlet Madder . . ,,	0	2	0
Malachite Green . ,,	0	2	0
Oxide of Chromium . ,,	0	2	0
Emerald ditto . . ,,	0	2	0
Yellow Madder, pale and deep . . . ,,	0	2	0
Ultramarine Grey . ,,	0	2	0
Extract of Vermilion ,,	0	2	0
Mars Orange . . . ,,	0	2	0
Lemon Yellow, pale and deep . . each	0	1	6
Mars Yellow . . . ,,	0	1	6
Strontian Yellow . ,,	0	1	6
French Ultramarine ,,	0	1	6
Cobalt Blue . . . ,,	0	1	6
Brown Madder . . ,,	0	1	6
Pink Madder . . . ,,	0	1	6
Rose Madder . . . ,,	0	1	6
Indian Yellow . . ,,	0	1	6
Orange Lake . . . ,,	0	1	6
Orange Vermilion . ,,	0	1	6
Vermilion . . . . ,,	0	1	0
Burnt Lake . . . ,,	0	0	9
Cerulium . . . . ,,	0	0	9

ROBERSON'S Crimson Lake, warranted to keep good, 9d.

VARNISHES, OILS, &c.
In Glass Bottles.

	Rounds.		½ Pints.		Pints.	
	s.	d.	s.	d.	s.	d.
Mastic Varnish	2	0	6	0	12	0
Preparation of Copal	1	3	4	0	8	0
Copal Oil Varnish	1	0	3	6	7	0
White Spirit or Spa ditto	1	0	3	6	7	0
Japan Gold Size	0	8	2	0	4	0
Nut Oil	1	0	2	0	4	0
Poppy Oil	0	8	1	6	3	0
Cold-drawn Linseed Oil	0	6	1	6	3	0
Pale Drying Oil	0	6	1	6	3	0
Rectified Spirits of Turpentine	0	6	1	3	2	6

ROBERSON'S MEDIUM FOR OIL PAINTING.

This Medium has now been in universal use by Artists for forty years, and is confidently recommended for its quality, of imparting permanency and richness to Colours.

IN TUBES,—(Size of Engraving) . . . . *each* 1s.
LARGER DITTO . . . . . . „ 1s. 6d.

Please observe that the neck of the Tube is stamped "ROBERSON'S MEDIUM."

Parris's Marble Medium in Tubes . *each* 1s. & 1s. 6d.

JAPANNED TIN OIL COLOUR BOXES.

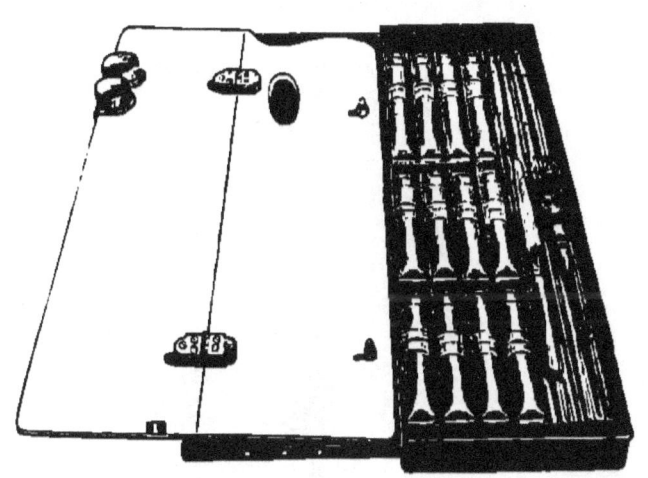

	Empty. £. s. d.	Fitted Complete. £. s. d.
Japanned Sketching Box, Twelve Tube Colours, Brushes and folding Palette, size 13¼ in. by 4¾ in. and 1¼ in. deep	0 6 0	1 5 0
Ditto, 1¾ in. deep, with Tray for extra Colours, larger assortment of Brushes, and portable Rest Stick	0 8 0	2 5 0
Japanned Box, Sixteen Tubes, Palette, Brushes, Oils, &c., size 10 in. by 6¾ in. and 2¼ deep .	0 9 0	1 16 0
Ditto. Twenty Tubes, Palette, Brushes, Oils, &c., size 10¾ in. by 7¾ in. and 2¾ in. deep . .	0 11 0	2 5 0
Ditto, Twenty-seven Tubes, Palette, Brushes, Oils, &c., size 13 in. by 8½ in. and 3 in. deep . .	0 13 0	3 10 0

OIL COLOUR BOXES,
CONTINUED.

	Empty. £. s. d.	Fitted Complete. £. s. d.
Japanned Tin Box for Twenty-seven Tubes, Palette, Brushes, Rest Stick, Oils, &c., with double bottom for Three Millboards, size 13½ in. by 9½ in. and 3½ in. deep	1 0 0	4 4 0

WALNUT-WOOD OIL COLOUR SKETCHING BOXES,

EMPTY WITH WHITE WOOD PANELS,

From 10s. 6d. to 35s.

FINE LINEN CANVAS, prepared for Oil Painting.

Prepared in a superior manner, in Canvas, Roman and Ticken.

¾ or 27 in. wide	per yard	3 feet 9 in. wide per yard
⅞ or 30 ,,	,,	4 ,, 6 ,, ,,
36 ,,	,,	5 ,, 2 ,, ,,
38 ,,	,,	6 ,, 2 ,, ,,
3 feet 6 ,,	,,	7 ,, 2 ,, ,,

PREPARED CANVAS ON FRAMES.

Portrait Sizes,
ON WEDGED FRAMES.

Inches.		£. s. d.
10 ,, 8	. . . . .	
12 ,, 10	. . . . .	
14 ,, 12	. . . . .	
16 ,, 14	. . . . .	
20 ,, 16	. . . . .	
21 ,, 17	. . . . .	
24 ,, 20, Head Size	. . .	
30 ,, 25, Three-quarter size	.	
36 ,, 28, Kitcat	. . .	
44 ,, 34, Small half-length	.	
50 ,, 40, Half-length	. .	
56 ,, 44, Bishop's Half-length	.	
7 ft. 10 by 4 ft. 10, Whole length	.	
8 ft. 10 by 5 ft. 10, Bishop's whole length	. . . .	

Landscape Sizes,
ON WEDGED FRAMES.

Inches.	£. s. d.
9 by 6 .	
10 ,, 7 .	
12 ,, 8 .	
12 ,, 9 .	
13 ,, 9 .	
14 ,, 10 .	
16 ,, 12 .	
18 ,, 12 .	
20 ,, 14 .	
24 ,, 18 .	
30 ,, 20 .	
36 ,, 24 .	
50 ,, 30 .	

PREPARED MILLBOARDS,
From 6 inches by 5 to 30 inches by 25.

SUPERIOR PANELS, prepared of well-seasoned Mahogany,
From 8 inches by 6 to 36 inches by 28.

PREPARED ACADEMY BOARDS.

PAPER for Sketching in Oil, also made in Blocks.

EXTRA FINE HOG HAIR BRUSHES.

In Tin, Flat and Round.

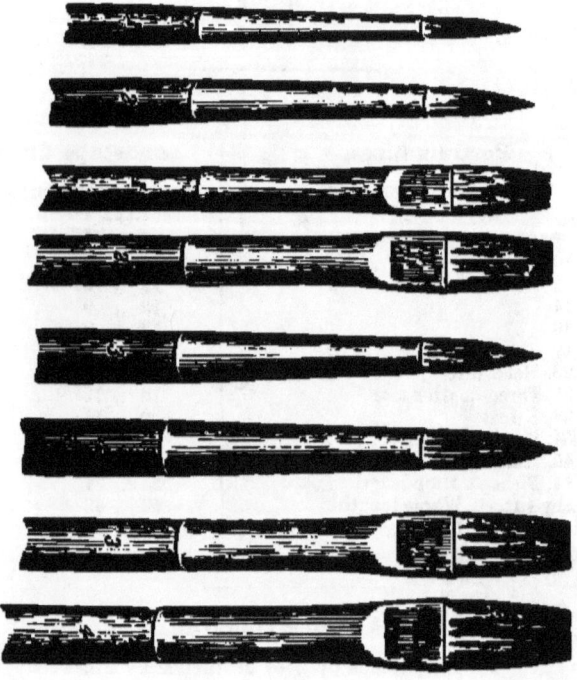

		s.	d.
No. 1	each	0	6
,, 2	,,	0	6
,, 3	,,	0	7
,, 4	,,	0	7
,, 5	,,	0	8
,, 6	,,	0	9
,, 7	,,	0	10
,, 8	,,	1	0

FLAT SABLE BRUSHES, in Tin, for OIL PAINTING.

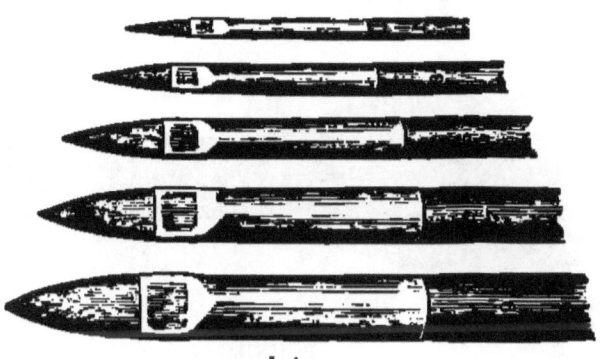

		s.	d.			s.	d.
No. 1	each	0	6	No. 7	each	1	9
,, 2	,,	0	8	,, 8	,,	2	0
,, 3	,,	0	10	,, 9	,,	2	6
,, 4	,,	1	0	,, 10	,,	3	0
,, 5	,,	1	3	,, 11	,,	3	6
,, 6	,,	1	6	,, 12	,,	4	0

ROUND SABLE BRUSHES, IN TIN, FOR OIL PAINTING.

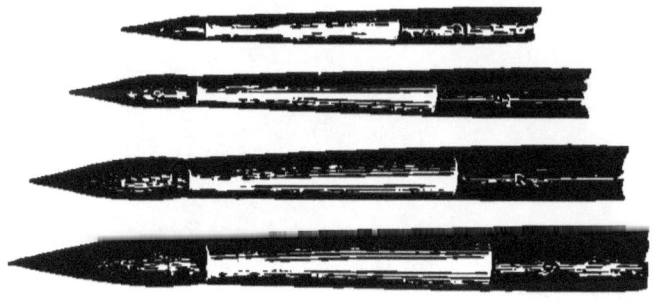

		s.	d.			s.	d.
No. 1	each	0	6	No. 6	each	1	6
,, 2	,,	0	8	,, 7	,,	2	0
,, 3	,,	0	10	,, 8	,,	2	3
,, 4	,,	1	0	,, 9	,,	3	0
,, 5	,,	1	3	,, 10	,,	4	0

CHARLES ROBERSON & CO.,

BADGER HAIR BRUSHES FOR SOFTENING, &c.

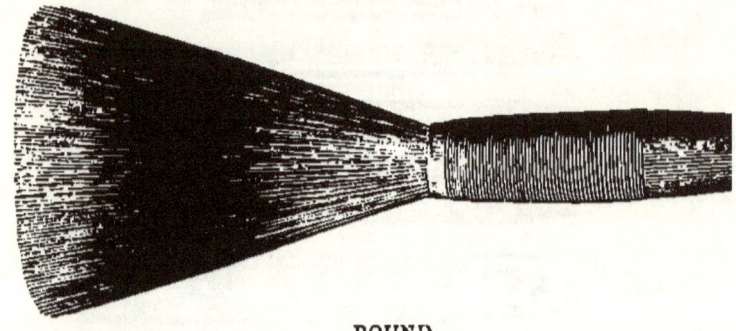

ROUND.

		s.	d.			s.	d.
No. 1	. each	0	8	No. 5	. each	2	6
,, 2	. ,,	1	0	,, 6	. ,,	3	0
,, 3	. ,,	1	3	,, 7	. ,,	3	6
,, 4	. ,,	1	9	,, 8	. ,,	4	0

FINE HOG HAIR FLAT BRUSHES FOR VARNISHING.

PALETTE KNIVES, &c.

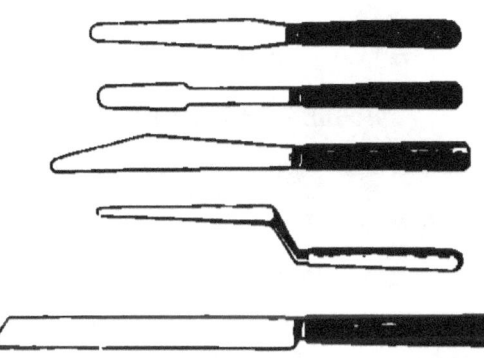

Steel Palette Knives (patterns as above) . . 9d. to 2s. 6d. each.
Ivory Palette Knives . . . . . . 1s. to 2s. 6d. ,,
Gilder's Knives . . . . . . 1s. 9d. to 2s. 6d. ,,
Artists' Pocket Knives for Erasing, &c., 2 blades . 2s. 6d. ,,

TIN DIPPERS FOR OIL.

		s.	d.
Plain Tin Dippers	each	0	4
Ditto, Double ditto	,,	0	6
Japanned Dippers, Single	,,	0	6
Ditto ditto, Double	,,	1	0

IMPROVED DIPPER, WITH RIM.

		s.	d.
Improved Japanned Tin Dippers, Small size	each	1	0
Ditto ditto Middle ,,	,,	1	3
Ditto ditto Large ,,	,,	1	6
Tin Plain Brush Washers	,,	1	6
Japanned ditto	,,	2	6
Tin Brush Pans, Small size	,,	3	6
Ditto Middle ,,	,,	4	0
Ditto Large ,,	,,	4	6

PARISIAN LAY FIGURES, latest improvements.

Life Size, Male, Female, or Child . . . each £

THE ABOVE LENT ON HIRE AT PER MONTH.

WOOLEN LAY FIGURES.

	£.	s.	d.
From 6 inches to 24 inches high . . each 3s. to	0	15	0
Ditto, Life Size	8	0	0
Lay Figure of Horse			

DRAWING MODELS IN WOOD.

Consisting of a large number of Solids, of simple forms, capable of being combined into a variety of figures, in boxes from 8s. to 2 2 0

MATERIALS FOR GILDING, &c.

		£	s	d
Oil Gold Size	per tube	0	1	0
Water ditto	per bottle	0	1	0
Fat Oil	per bottle	0	1	0
Burnish Gold Size	per tube	0	0	6
Japanner's Gold Size	per bottle	0	0	8
Gilder's Cushions	each	0	3	0
Ditto Tips	„	0	0	4
Ditto Knives	each, 1s. 9d. to	0	2	6
Ditto Burnishers	„ 2s. 6d. to	0	3	6
Gold Leaf	per book	0	2	0
Silver ditto	„	0	1	6

PALETTES—Mahogany, Sycamore and Satinwood.
Also to fold.

Pictures carefully Lined, Cleaned, Repaired and Varnished, Panels Parqueted.

ETCHING & COPPER PLATE PRINTING MATERIALS.

		£.	s.	d.
Burnishers, finest steel	from	0	1	6
Blotting Paper	per quire	0	2	0
Bordering Wax	per stick	0	1	0
Copper Plates	from	0	1	0
Boxes for ditto		0	2	0
Charcoal, Vine and Willow	per dozen sticks	0	1	0
Dabbers, Silk	each	0	2	0
Ditto, Leather	„	0	2	0
Etching Needles	„	0	0	6
Ditto, fixed in handles	from	0	1	6
Ditto, all steel	„	0	1	0
Ditto, double ends	„	0	1	6
Emery Cloth and Powder				
Etching Ground	per ball	0	1	0
Ditto, Liquid	per bottle	0	1	0
Gravers and Handles				
Handvices, with Handles	each			
Imitation India Paper, white and toned	per sheet	0	0	8
Printing Presses, with Blanket and Cloth	each	3	3	0
Ditto, large size „ „	„	5	5	0
Porcelain Baths	„	0	1	6
Trays for ditto				
Palette Knives	from each	0	1	0
Plate Paper, White and Toned	per sheet	0	0	8
Printing Ink	per bottle	0	1	0
Reducing Oil	per bottle	0	0	6
Stopping Out Varnish	„	0	1	0
Transparent Varnish	„	0	1	0
Scrapers, finest steel	from	0	2	6
Spirit Lamps	from each	0	1	6
Tracing Paper	from per sheet	0	0	4
Tapers				
Tripoli Powder				

BOXES OF ETCHING MATERIALS complete, including Printing Press, (*see page* 31),

From £5. 5s. 0d. to £8. 8s. 0d. each.

LIQUID INK FOR PEN AND INK DRAWING.

1s. 6d. per bottle.

Crow Quill Pens and Quills,

6d. per dozen.

Lithographic Crow Quill Pens,

2s. 6d. per card of 12.

LITHOGRAPHIC CHALKS AND INKS.

BOX WOOD BLOCKS AND MATERIALS FOR ENGRAVERS.

PUBLICATIONS BY ROBERSON & CO.

THE ETCHER'S HAND-BOOK,

By PHILIP GILBERT HAMERTON, author of "Etchings and Etchers." Illustrated by the Author. Price 5s.

THE PROPORTIONS OF THE HUMAN FIGURE,

As handed down to us by VITRUVIUS; to which is added the Method of Measuring the Figure, invented by JOHN GIBSON, Sculptor. With Description and Illustrative Outlines by JOSEPH BONOMI, F.R.A.S., M.S.B.A., Curator Sir John Soane's Museum. Price 2s.

A New Edition, just Published. 2s.

HAND-BOOK OF ANATOMY FOR ARTISTS.

By J. A. WHEELER. With Illustrations.

BOXES OF ETCHING MATERIALS complete, including Printing Press, (*see page* 31),

From £5. 5s. 0d. to £8. 8s. 0d. each.

LIQUID INK FOR PEN AND INK DRAWING.

1s. 6d. per bottle.

Crow Quill Pens and Quills,

6d. per dozen.

Lithographic Crow Quill Pens,

2s. 6d. per card of 12.

LITHOGRAPHIC CHALKS AND INKS.

BOX WOOD BLOCKS AND MATERIALS FOR ENGRAVERS.

PUBLICATIONS BY ROBERSON & CO.

THE ETCHER'S HAND-BOOK,

By PHILIP GILBERT HAMERTON, author of "Etchings and Etchers." Illustrated by the Author. Price 5s.

THE PROPORTIONS OF THE HUMAN FIGURE,

As handed down to us by VITRUVIUS; to which is added the Method of Measuring the Figure, invented by JOHN GIBSON, Sculptor. With Description and Illustrative Outlines by JOSEPH BONOMI, F.R.A.S., M.S.B.A., Curator Sir John Soane's Museum. Price 2s.

A New Edition, just Published. 2s.

HAND-BOOK OF ANATOMY FOR ARTISTS.

By J. A. WHEELER. With Illustrations.

www.ingramcontent.com/pod-product-compliance
Lightning Source LLC
Chambersburg PA
CBHW030337170426
43202CB00010B/1160